THE STORY OF PAUL III

OF

THE FINAL YEARS

BY TREVOR GALPIN

Copyright 2023

The Story of Paul III - The Final Years
by Trevor Galpin

Published by TLG Mins (US) Inc

Design and Layout by Tom Carroll
Edited by Felicia Murrell

Printed by IngramSpark & Amazon

ISBN: 978-1-8380570-8-4

All rights reserved. No part of this publication may be reproduced, stored in a retrieval system or transmitted in any form or by any means - for example, electronic, photocopy, recording - without the prior written permission of the author or publisher. The only exception is brief quotation in printed reviews.

All Scripture quotations, unless otherwise indicated, are taken from The Holy Bible, New International Version®, NIV® Copyright ©1973, 1978, 1984, 2011 by Biblica, Inc.®. Used by permission. All rights reserved worldwide.

For more information and resources by Trevor and Linda Galpin please visit: **www.trevorandlinda.uk**

INTRODUCTION

It had to come one day and here it is, *The Story of Paul III the Final Years*.

This book was much harder to write than I thought it would be. The reason being, there are so few historical facts to work with. Luke writes about Paul in his final chapters of *The Acts of the Apostles*. Yet his main purpose for writing is to show how the Gospel was taken to Rome rather than the events of Paul's life. Luke gives us fascinating details particularly when he was personally present, such as in the shipwreck on the Island of Malta. He neatly concludes Acts with Paul a free man in Rome. Traditions of the church claim Paul was beheaded by Nero in Rome. Fanciful legend says his head bounced three times and three fountains miraculously appeared out of the ground. But was he beheaded? Indeed, was he beheaded in Rome even? For information of Paul's death, we are dependent on early traditions from the second and third century, about when, where, and how. Nothing is certain. In reality, solid evidence is virtually non-existent.

What about Paul's prison letters? Traditionally, they were thought to have been written from a supposed Roman imprisonment. But Luke does not have him in prison in Rome. If you have read my book *The Story of Paul II - the Middle Years*, you may recall I think Paul wrote them from a time in prison in Ephesus. I am in good company with

INTRODUCTION

some of the most eminent biblical scholars on this one. Paul's three pastoral letters to Timothy and Titus do however reflect a time at the end of Paul's life after the close of Acts. They contain tantalising clues about his travels and a possible fourth missionary journey after the close of Acts 28.

Unpicking the so called fourth missionary journey as suggested by the pastorals is at best tricky and every commentator has their own version, for example, N.T. Wright describes the summary of Paul's final years by the leading Roman Catholic authority on Paul, Jerome Murphy-O'Connor, as a 'novella'. I am therefore in good company. Summarising Paul's final years is like trying to do a jigsaw with no picture.

What are we left with? A few crumbs from Luke, a few titbits from Paul, and the notoriously unreliable traditions of the early centuries of the church. This is why I have wondered whether I should even attempt writing this book. But I couldn't let it rest. I felt it reaching out to me and the challenge appealed to my fertile imagination as storyteller. I found myself again asking questions such as, "So what did Luke do while Paul was in prison for two years in Caesarea?" Did Paul ever make it to Spain as he hoped? Clement of Rome, writing sixty years after Paul's death, said Paul 'went to the farthest reaches of the west.' Did he mean Spain? Did Paul die in Rome, and was he martyred?

The outcome once again, like *The Story of Paul II the Middle Years*, is a fictive historical narrative. As a storyteller, does one merely need to fill in the blanks? If so, it is something I want to attempt in a historically reliable way. In the end, if I am brutally honest, it turned out to be more fictional than I had intended because of the paucity of historical evidence.

INTRODUCTION

I enjoyed attempting to fill in the blanks. I enjoyed developing some of the characters Paul met along the way: Julius the Centurion who escorts him on the ill-fated voyage to Rome and Paul's fourth shipwreck. Lysias, the commander of the garrison in Jerusalem, became a binding thread. Then, there is the enigmatic Lucina; a woman we know nothing about. She turns up as a one liner from the fourth century, *Liber Pontificalis,* which states Paul's body was buried outside the walls of Rome, at the second mile on the Via Ostiensis, on the estate owned by a Christian woman named Lucina. This is far too tempting to not bring her into the story.

As before, I have tried to avoid using the word "church" because we have such a twenty-first century model of church in our minds. I try to describe the activities and relationships of believers rather than use the generic word. Likewise, with the word Christian, which was not widely used in the first century. Where the action can be found in the Bible I have added a numbered note which are all listed at the end.

And finally, this book, like all the other books I have written, is ultimately about the revelation of God as Father who wants to have relationship with his sons and daughters. Fictive storytelling allows me the privilege of exploring this in a human context through the way the characters interact and behave and what I imagine they say as they try to come to terms with the amazing revelation that God the Father was in Christ reconciling the world to himself.

I found myself shedding a tear at the end as Paul is laid to rest. I felt I was bidding farewell to a dear friend. This is not a spoiler as such because I presume everyone knows Paul finally died.

So here it is, *The Story of Paul III - the Final Years.* I hope you enjoy it!

CONTENTS

Introduction	V
Chapter I	10
Chapter II	27
Chapter III	63
Chapter IV	86
Chapter V	98
Chapter VI	107
Chapter VII	113
Chapter VIII	133
Chapter IX	141
Chapter X	150
Chapter XI	159
Chapter XII	169
Chapter XIII	181
Chapter XIV	195
Chapter XV	206
Chapter XVI	224
Possible route of Paul's last journey	239
Dramatis Personae	240
Notes	254
Other Books by Trevor Galpin	259
Resources	263

CHAPTER I

Tribune Claudius Lysias stood staring out of the window of his office in the Antonia Fortress high above the Jerusalem temple. Below, in the precincts of the temple complex, shouting of rioting Jews swelled. As commander of the Roman garrison in Jerusalem, for a little over two years, the last thing he needed was another riot and more bloodshed in the city.

The place was always a tinder box and trouble could break out at any time with these tiresome Jews. There had been a steady increase in attacks on the Roman occupiers by the fanatical Zealots over recent years. Lysias had lost count of the number of troops who died in street attacks. He stopped counting the number of executions and crucifixions he had authorized as a result. He was sickened by the bloodshed and continual pressure of the position of commander of the Roman garrison. The posting was considered one of the worst anyone could be given in the whole empire. He hated this place. He hated the Jews. He particularly hated their fanatical religious hierarchy who thought they controlled the city and the province. He hated the fact this was probably true.

The previous day had been yet another example of this when a riot broke out in the temple. A Jew from the provinces had somehow offended the Temple leadership. As usual, they plotted and connived

CHAPTER 1

to create an incident to involve the Roman authorities in an attempt to get Lysias to do their dirty work.

Yesterday morning as the sun's first rays broke across the city rising above the hills to the east, Lysias could hear the commotion. The whole city seemed to be stirred up and people were pouring in from all directions. There was shouting, stone throwing and fights breaking out. Several soldiers were caught by the mob and badly beaten. Lysias would have to do something to try to calm things down.

After a knock on his door, an officer entered and informed the commander the crowd had seized a man and dragged him from the temple and shut the gates of the temple so they could kill him outside the holy precincts. Lysias sighed, went down the steps to the entry of the fortress with some officers and soldiers to confront the crowd. As soon as the rioters saw the commander and his soldiers, they stopped beating the man. On approaching the bloodied man, Lysias ordered the soldiers to seize him and bind him with chains. This calmed the crowd and Lysias called for silence.[1]

"Who is this man and what has he done?" Lysias demanded.

People in the crowd started shouting. Some shouted one thing and others another. It was clear to Lysias he would not get the truth, so he ordered the soldiers to take the man into the barracks. When they reached the steps, the mob surged forward, and violence erupted again forcing the soldiers to carry the man on their shoulders to avoid him being attacked. The crowd was baying for his blood and for him to be killed. The soldiers had reached the barrack doors when the unfortunate man, now back on his feet, turned and spoke to the commander,

"May I say something to you?"

"You speak Greek!" Lysias replied. "Aren't you the Egyptian who started a revolt and led four thousand terrorists out into the wilderness some time ago?"

"What? Not me. My name is Paul. I am a Jew from Tarsus in Cilicia, a citizen of no ordinary city. Please let me speak to the people."

Lysias realised, yet again, the information fed to him by the Jewish religious authorities was totally inaccurate. Lysias agreed to let him speak, thinking if the people found out this man was not an Egyptian terrorist but a Jew like them, things would settle down and hopefully the rioters would disperse. Little did he realise what would ensue once Paul began to speak.[2]

The soldiers flanked Paul as he stood on the steps and waved to try to get the crowd to be quiet. When they finally settled, he addressed them in Aramaic:

"Brothers and fathers, listen to my defence."

Hearing Paul speaking in Aramaic, the crowd stilled. Unable to understand the language, Lysias was mystified. With no idea what the man was saying, he called for a translator to come and tell him what was happening. He watched the crowd intensely and tried to catch words from the man called Paul.

Paul continued.

"I am a Jew, born in Tarsus of Cilicia, but brought up in this city. I studied under Gamaliel and was thoroughly trained in the law of our ancestors. I was just as zealous for God as any of you are today. I persecuted the followers of the Way to their death, arresting both men and women and throwing them into prison, as the high priest and all the Council can themselves testify. I even obtained letters

CHAPTER 1

from them to their associates in Damascus and went there to bring these people as prisoners to Jerusalem to be punished."

Some of the older ones listening began to remember back to those days and several looked at one another and commented,

"I recognise him. Isn't this man's real name Saul from Tarsus? He was one of the best Pharisees to come out of Gamaliel's school years ago. What is he talking about now?"

"Yes, I think it is him. I haven't heard of him for years. Some time ago, he reappeared and declared himself a follower of the Nazarene heretic Jesus," said another.

"Shush, you two! Shut up! Let's hear what he has to say," said another man.

"About noon, as I came near Damascus," Paul continued, "suddenly a bright light from heaven flashed around me. I fell to the ground and heard a voice say to me, 'Saul! Saul! Why do you persecute me?'

"'Who are you, Lord?' I asked.

"'I am Jesus of Nazareth, whom you are persecuting,' he replied. My companions saw the light, but they did not understand the voice of the one who was speaking to me.

"'What shall I do, Lord?' I asked.

"'Get up,' the Lord said, 'and go into Damascus. There you will be told all that you have been assigned to do.' My companions led me by the hand into Damascus, because the brilliance of the light blinded me.

"A man named Ananias came to see me. He was a devout observer of the law and highly respected by all the Jews living there. He stood beside me and said, 'Brother Saul, receive your sight!' And at that exact moment, I was able to see him.

"Then he said: 'The God of our ancestors has chosen you to know his will and to see the Righteous One and to hear words from his mouth. You will be his witness to all people of what you have seen and heard. And now what are you waiting for? Get up, be baptized, and wash your sins away, calling on his name.'"

Many in the crowd began to murmur and were not happy with what Paul was saying.

"Who do you think you are? Talking about the 'Righteous one' like this," someone shouted.

"Blasphemer!" shouted another.

The mention of the name of Jesus of Nazareth incited the crowd. Some began to shout insults at him. Unconcerned, Paul pressed on with his story.

"When I returned to Jerusalem and was praying at the temple, I fell into a trance and saw the Lord speaking to me. 'Quick!' he said. 'Leave Jerusalem immediately, because the people here will not accept your testimony about me.'

"'Lord,' I replied, 'these people know that I went from one synagogue to another to imprison and beat those who believe in you. And when the blood of your martyr Stephen was shed, I stood there giving my approval and guarding the clothes of those who were killing him.'

"Then the Lord said to me, 'Go; I will send you far away to the Gentiles.'"

This was too much for the crowd. His mention of going to the

CHAPTER 1

Gentiles infuriated them. They started shouting and yelling insults.

"Gentile lover!"

"Rid the earth of him! He's not fit to live!"[3]

The shouting became deafening. They started throwing off their cloaks and flinging dust into the air. This was too much and Lysias ordered for Paul to be taken into the barracks. Once inside he wasn't sure what to do so he ordered Paul to be flogged and interrogated in order to find out why the people were shouting at him like this. The soldiers stripped him naked and tied him to a post ready to have him flogged. When they tore off his tunic, Lysias gasped at the numerous scars across Paul's back. Bile filled his mouth. This Paul was a man who had obviously endured many beatings. Lysias turned to the centurion in charge.

"Just get on with it, but don't kill him."

With that, Lysias walked up the stairs to his office. He had seen enough blood for one day. He went into his office, grabbed a bowl and vomited into it.

Below in the courtyard, Paul spoke to the centurion standing there, overseeing the flogging.

"Is it legal for you to flog a Roman citizen who hasn't even been found guilty?"

When the centurion heard this, he ordered the soldier who was about to flog Paul to wait and went to the commander himself.

"Commander," he said. "This man claims he is a Roman citizen. What do you want me to do?"

Lysias splashed water on his face and went down the stairs again to Paul.

THE STORY OF PAUL III

"Tell me, are you a Roman citizen?"

"Yes, I am," said Paul.

Lysias stared with astonishment at the naked man tied to the whipping post in front of him claiming to be a Roman citizen. He was confused. *How could this man be a citizen, he doesn't look Roman?* Lysias' head was spinning. It felt like he was losing his grip on the situation. With indignation, he remarked to Paul.

"I had to pay a lot of money for my citizenship."

"But I was born a citizen," Paul replied.

This changed everything. If this were true, Paul outranked the commander and to have him flogged because of the whim of the mob would be a bad mistake for Lysias. The centurion and those who were about to interrogate Paul quickly withdrew not wishing to be implicated in the possible mistake.

"Untie him immediately and put his clothes back on," commanded Lysias.

Lysias became alarmed as he grasped the situation. He had put Paul, a Roman citizen by birth, in chains and ordered him to be flogged without trial or making serious enquiry. Another error of judgement on his part. Another mistake to explain or cover up. The last thing Lysias wanted was the Provincial Governor Felix hearing about this and posting him down to the Negev or some other dust bowl as punishment. There was no love lost between Lysias and Felix. Lysias needed to find out exactly why Paul was being accused by the Jews. He decided to let things settle overnight. After Paul was unchained, Lysias had him moved to Antonia Fortress for his safety.[4]

The following day, Lysias left his quarters and went down to the

CHAPTER 1

audience chamber in the Antonia Fortress. He was not in a good mood and wanted to resolve the problem as quickly as possible.

He brought Paul out and sent an order for the chief priests and all the members of the Sanhedrin to assemble. When the council arrived outside the Antonia, they refused to enter the fortress on the pretext of not wanting to contaminate themselves by entering the defiled Roman and Gentile fortress. Lysias brought out Paul and had him stand before them. They were also angry at seeing Paul standing there next to the commander and his soldiers. They pressed forward and were soon close to Paul. Lysias commanded them to be quiet and when they finally quietened down, Lysias turned to Paul.

"Explain yourself and keep it brief. I haven't got all day."

Paul looked intently at the faces in front of him. Some of them, he recognised from his youth many years ago in Jerusalem. They had aged as had he. He noticed some younger sterner faces. They were a new generation of Pharisees and scribes he did not know.

"My brothers," he began. "I have fulfilled my duty to God in all good conscience to this day."

In the crowd was the aging High Priest Ananias who ordered those standing near Paul to punch him on the mouth. The blow took him by surprise, and he staggered back as blood poured out of his mouth.

"God will strike you," Paul immediately replied spitting blood. "You whitewashed wall! You sit there to judge me according to the law, yet you yourself violate the law by commanding I be struck!"

"How dare you insult God's high priest!" shouted one of the Council.

"Stop that immediately!" Lysias interrupted. "Anyone who touches this man will feel the steel of my sword."

He drew it for good measure as the angry Council members stepped back out of range.

"Brothers," continued Paul, "I did not realise he was the high priest; I would not have spoken evil about the ruler of your people if I had known."

Paul knew some of them were Sadducees and others, Pharisees, so he shouted loudly so they could all hear him,

"My brothers, I am a Pharisee, descended from Pharisees. I stand on trial because of the hope of the resurrection of the dead."

Paul knew exactly what reaction this statement would have on the council. Immediately, arguments broke out between the Pharisees and the Sadducees. The assembly was divided between Sadducees who did not believe in resurrection, nor angels or spirits, and Pharisees who believed in all these things. There was a great uproar, and some of the teachers of the law who were Pharisees started to argue vigorously.

"We find nothing wrong with this man," they shouted. "What if a spirit or an angel has spoken to him?"

The dispute became so violent, Lysias was afraid they would tear Paul to pieces. Scuffles were breaking out between the Council members, so he ordered his soldiers to take Paul away and return him to the fortress. Once inside the safety of the fortress, Lysias ordered his troops to secure the gates and he commanded Paul to come to his private suite of rooms.

Paul walked into the well-appointed and comfortable chamber.

CHAPTER 1

The windows were covered by gauze drapes which allowed the breeze to blow into the room. Paul stood there wiping blood from his chin and face.

"Sit!" Lysias ordered as he poured himself a goblet of wine. "I will get a slave to bring you water. Do you want a drink? When did you last eat? Or am I too unclean for you to eat a Greek's food?"

Paul was hungry and eagerly nodded. The commander's words had amazed him and he had suspected the commander was Greek since his accent placed him as a Greek rather than a Roman. He was also surprised at the hint of kindness in the man's voice. He thought the commander a man of contradictions.

Lysias watched Paul hungrily devour the food and drink the good Cypriot wine brought to him.

"Why do they hate you so much? Why are they trying to kill you?"

Paul looked at Lysias. The man tried to sound severe but he was displaying genuine interest. Paul did not answer the question, instead he commented.

"I don't envy your job, so far from your home." He took another mouthful of wine.

"What makes you think I am far from home?"

"Your accent sounds Macedonian to me," replied Paul.

"How would you know that?" Lysias was somewhat surprised.

"I know Macedonia well; I've been there many times."

Lysias studied Paul's face as if he was trying to decide what to make of the man. Then he said,

"I'm originally from Philippi. My father was a wealthy merchant in the city and became a freedman. We owe our freedom to a member of the Claudian family, hence my name Claudius Lysias. I joined the army and I have done well. I eventually bought my citizenship, and I was then promoted to Military Tribune. This is my first posting."

Speaking of his achievements seemed to elicit pride in his voice.

"My father died recently. But I have not been back to Philippi or seen my mother and family for some time."

"I have spent time in Philippi, over the last few years, and I have many friends there," added Paul.

"Who do you know in the city?" asked Lysias.

"One of my closest friends and travelling companions is from there. He is a Greek doctor."

"Really? What is his name?" asked Lysias.

"Lucas. He was once a physician in Philippi."

Lysias looked surprised. "I knew a man called Lucas. He was a friend of mine when I was younger. I wonder if it is the same person. I haven't seen him for many years." His face contorted as he tried to hide his emotions then he continued,

"Who else do you know there?"

"Well, a dear friend is also a merchant, a dealer in purple. A woman originally from Thyatira. Her name is Lydia."[5]

Lysias' mouth dropped open and he took a large gulp of wine. He rubbed his hand across his face, then looked at Paul.

"Lydia is my aunt," said Lysias.

Paul stared in amazement and smiled at Lysias.

CHAPTER 1

"It seems we have been brought together for some reason, Lysias. Lucas is here in Judea, maybe even in the city. But if he is not here, he is probably down in Caesarea."

Lysias stood and walked to the window. He gazed out across the city; his mind was in turmoil. Then he turned to Paul.

"I will have a room prepared for you. It's not fancy, but you will be safe there… at least for tonight. Go now with this servant. We will talk tomorrow and see what the new day brings."

Paul stood and looked at Lysias again. He saw the muscles working in the man's jaw and detected a moistening of his eyes. He wondered what was going on in the man.

As Paul lay down to sleep, he felt in his spirit the unexpected encounter with Lysias was more significant than he could ever have imagined. He hoped he would have the chance to tell Lucas of this soon. Paul felt the presence of Jesus in the room with him. He felt Jesus say to him,

"Take courage! As you have testified about me in Jerusalem, so you must also testify in Rome." Then Paul, at peace, drifted off to sleep.[6]

Unknown to Paul, a conspiracy was being hatched among some of the Jews who bound themselves with an oath not to eat or drink until they killed Paul. More than forty men were involved in this plot. They had gone to the chief priests and the elders and informed them of their plan to kill Paul.

They asked the High Priest to petition the commander to bring Paul to the Sanhedrin to appear before them on the pretext of wanting more accurate information about his case. They planned to attack Paul on the way and kill him before he got to the High Priest's house.

THE STORY OF PAUL III

The plot was not a well-kept secret. Paul's nephew, who lived in Jerusalem with his mother, Paul's sister, was told about the plot by a former Pharisee who now considered himself a follower of Jesus but was opposed to Paul's teaching and activity among the Gentiles. The man encouraged the boy to go and inform Paul. As soon as the boy heard this, he went straight to the fortress and asked to see Paul on the pretext of bringing him food from his mother.[7]

Arriving at the fortress, he banged on the door used by those bringing food to the prisoners. He told the guard he had bread for the prisoner Paul and was let in. Within a few minutes he was standing in front of Paul.

"Uncle, I have bread for you." The boy was out of breath and agitated.

"Calm down, lad, and tell me whatever is the matter," said Paul. "Is all well with your mother?"

The whole story tumbled out. Paul knew who had sent the message. He needed to act fast and called the centurion.

"Take this young man to the commander; he has something important to tell him."

The soldier agreed and took the lad to the commander.

"Paul, the Jewish prisoner, sent for me and asked me to bring this young man to you. He has information to tell you."

The commander took the young boy by the hand, drew him aside and asked,

"What is it you want to tell me?"

Being in the presence of the commander frightened the boy and he started to tremble.

CHAPTER 1

"Speak up, boy, don't be afraid. What is so important to make Paul send you to me?"

The boy summoned his courage,

"Some Jews are going to ask you to bring Paul before the Sanhedrin on the pretext of wanting more accurate information about him. Paul says you must not give in to them. More than forty of them will be waiting in ambush for him. They have taken an oath not to eat or drink until they have killed him. They are ready now, waiting for you to consent to their request."

The commander listened, then warned the boy.

"Don't tell anyone you have reported this to me. Leave it to me. You have done the right thing. Go home and keep out of the streets."[8]

Lysias knew he needed to act quickly. Paul was a Roman citizen. If he was murdered in Jerusalem under Lysias' protection, it would not reflect well on his authority as commander. He was already feeling insecure about his ability to command the garrison.

The second issue for Lysias was Paul himself. Since his first encounter with the man, he felt a strange connection with him. He had allowed himself to become personally involved, shared personal information with a prisoner only to discover they had mutual friends. Something was going on internally within Lysias' mind and heart which he couldn't define.

An elaborate plan formed in his mind. He called two of his centurions and gave them specific orders. They were to assemble their two centuries, two hundred men. Then also saddle up seventy horsemen and two hundred spearmen and march them to Caesarea at nine the same evening. A horse would be provided for Paul, and he would be placed among the horsemen.

The soldiers were due to go to Antipatris within the next few days and a detachment from the garrison there was due to be sent to Jerusalem. This plan would bring the scheduled troop movement forward and not draw any attention. The horsemen would continue to Caesarea. Under cover of these manoeuvres, Lysias would be able to ensure Paul's safe arrival to Governor Felix.

He decided to write a letter to Felix explaining why Paul was being sent. The facts were not exactly true, but he felt it covered his own back as far as Paul's arrest was concerned.

He called for a scribe and dictated a letter.

Claudius Lysias,

To His Excellency, Governor Felix:

Greetings.

This man was seized by the Jews, and they were about to kill him, but I came with my troops and rescued him, for I learned that he is a Roman citizen. I wanted to know why they were accusing him, so I brought him to their Sanhedrin. I found that the accusation had to do with questions about their law, but there was no charge against him that deserved death or imprisonment. When I was informed of a plot to be carried out against the man, I sent him to you at once. I also ordered his accusers to present to you their case against him.

The plan was put into action and Paul was secretly smuggled out of the Antonia Fortress under cover of darkness. The soldiers, carrying out their orders, took Paul with them and brought him as

CHAPTER 1

far as Antipatris. The next day, they let the cavalry go on with him. When the cavalry arrived in Caesarea, they delivered the letter to the governor and handed Paul over to him. No one in Jerusalem, except Lysias, knew where Paul had been taken.[9]

Felix, Governor of the Roman province of Judaea, was in his summer residence at Caesarea Maritima. The officer in command of the cavalry unit brought a rather dishevelled Paul with him into the governor's presence and handed the letter to him. Felix groaned when the letter from the commander of the garrison in Jerusalem was handed to him. Unimpressed with Lysias and his ability to maintain law order in Jerusalem, Felix knew the letter contained bad news. He had been actively looking for an excuse to move Lysias to a less demanding position. A letter from the ineffective commander was the last thing he wanted to think about.

"Oh! For Jupiter's sake!" declared Felix after he read the letter.

"Why on earth did that idiot Lysias send a whole cavalry unit down here just to deliver one prisoner, even if he is a Roman?"

The cavalry commander shrugged his shoulders hoping there would be no more questions and he would not have to explain about the two hundred troops left on Antipatris.

Felix looked at Paul, wrinkling his nose at the dirty blood-stained man in front of him.

"What province are you from?"

"I am a Roman citizen from the noble city of Tarsus in Cilicia," answered Paul.

With a look of disdain, Felix sniffed.

"I will hear your case when your accusers get here."

He then shouted,

"Guard! Take this man to Herod's palace. He has space there to house him but keep him under guard. I don't want him disappearing."

The guard took Paul and marched him off to Herod's palace.

Felix turned to the cavalry officer,

"As for you, go back to Jerusalem and take a letter to Lysias. I'm sick of that idiot's bungling. I am making you the new commander of the garrison at the Antonia. Claudius Lysias can go and sulk in Tiberius. It will all be in the letter and tell someone in the Jewish Council I have this man here and they had better send his accusers so I can sort this out. Get out of my sight and send in my scribe. The letter will be ready in an hour."[10]

CHAPTER II

One of the earliest followers of Jesus, Zacchaeus had lived in Caesarea for several years. He first met Jesus when the rabbi was passing through his hometown of Jericho. Zacchaeus was the chief tax collector when a bizarre encounter with Jesus transformed his life. After news began to circulate of Jesus' crucifixion and apparent resurrection, Zacchaeus left Jericho and moved to Jerusalem. There, he attached himself to the group of Jesus' followers in the city. He found a kindred spirit with one of the other close followers, a man named Matthew who had also been a tax collector.[11]

Zacchaeus was present, along with many others, when the risen Jesus appeared to them on one occasion. He estimated there had been many as five hundred gathered. A few weeks later, he was also present when an astonishing event took place early one morning in Jerusalem.

Many years later, Zacchaeus described the events to Lucas, one of Paul's close travelling companions who had accompanied him to Judaea, along with a group of others, carrying the collection made for the poor believers in Jerusalem.

"Early on the day of Pentecost, around the third hour, we were all together in the usual place at John Mark's mother's house. She had a large upstairs room where we often used to meet. We had been meeting like this since the last time we saw Jesus."

"The same place Jesus used on Passover night?" asked Lucas.

"The same," Zacchaeus replied.

"Suddenly, there was a strange sound like the blowing of a violent wind coming from heaven. It seemed to fill the whole house. Then, we saw what seemed to be flames of fire separating and hovering over us all and finally coming to rest on each one of us."

Zacchaeus paused as the memory flooded his mind.

"It was the Spirit of God as promised by Jesus. I am convinced it was the Spirit. All of us were filled with God's holy Spirit and we began to sing and shout and speak in languages we had never ever learned. It was absolutely amazing. I've never been the same since."[12]

That was the beginning of a new life for Zacchaeus. Some years later, he moved to Caesarea and joined Philip, one of the leaders originally from Jerusalem, in encouraging the growing group of followers of Jesus in the city. Now, nearly twenty-eight years later, as an older man, he was loved and held in great respect by the community in Caesarea and considered as one of their first leaders.[13]

News had reached the believers in Caesarea of Paul's arrest in Jerusalem, and they were anxiously waiting for further information. About a week later, a messenger came to Zacchaeus from Philip asking him to come to his home as there were important developments.

Zacchaeus made his way to Philip's house and joined the other leaders, which included a former Roman centurion called Cornelius, a man named Theophilus and two of Philip's daughters.

"What's happened?" Zacchaeus asked.

CHAPTER II

Philip quickly reported the recent events as far as he knew them.

"As you know, Paul and a group of his friends from Asia and Greece had recently arrived from Macedonia and had gone up to Jerusalem with the gift they had collected for the poor in the community in Jerusalem. It was safely delivered into James's hands and the safe keeping of the leaders. Then, it seems, Paul was recognised by a group of Hellenistic Jews from the province of Asia who were also visiting Jerusalem. They apparently accused him of defiling the temple by bringing one of his Gentile friends into the precincts and being a blasphemer who taught against the Law of Moses. I seriously doubt Paul would have done this; he has more sense than to take a Gentile into the temple precincts."

"I remember Agabus warned him something might happen when he was here," said Zacchaeus.

"Indeed," continued Philip. "In the commotion, he was attacked and was being beating when one of the Roman guards intervened and discovered Paul was a Roman citizen. He was taken into custody for his own safety, and various hearings were held involving the Sanhedrin. Then a plot to kill him emerged." Philip paused before continuing.

"However, Paul's nephew, who lives in Jerusalem with his mother, heard of the plot and reported it to his uncle at the Roman barracks. We are not sure what exactly happened, but it seems the Roman commander ordered a detachment of guards to move him down here to Caesarea under the cover of night for his safety. He arrived in the early hours of this morning."

"So, now he is here in the governor's custody?" asked Cornelius.

"Yes," Philip nodded. "This morning I received news from

someone I know in the governor's residence who was present when a letter was delivered to the governor from the commander of the garrison in Jerusalem. More to the point, Paul was with them, and he has been handed over to Felix. The governor apparently read the letter and asked what province Paul was from. When he heard he came from Cilicia, Felix said he would wait to hear his case when his accusers arrive. Now he has placed Paul under guard in Herod's palace, of all places, and not in the governor's residence."

"It sounds to me, Felix is trying to avoid taking responsibility. Herod Agrippa hardly ever comes down here these days. Paul could be in there for weeks," said Cornelius.

"We need to get somebody in to see him. If he has been beaten up, we will need to get Lucas down here," added Zacchaeus.

"We must send word to Paul's friends in Jerusalem immediately as they may be in danger. A group of Gentiles in Jerusalem won't go unnoticed for long," said Cornelius. "I presume they are staying at Mnason's house?"

Philip nodded.

The plan rapidly came together. One of Philip's daughters and Zacchaeus went to Herod's palace to locate Paul. Cornelius dispatched a rider to Jerusalem to find Paul's friends and bring them down to Caesarea. Word was also sent to James to inform him of Paul's whereabouts.

As soon as Paul's travelling companions in Jerusalem learned of his fate, they hurriedly left for Caesarea. After arriving the next day, they went to Philip's house to discuss with the leaders what to do . A large group gathered in his home. Eight of them, including Timothy, Tychicus, Trophimus and Lucas, had brought the gift

CHAPTER II

from the Greek believers.

Zacchaeus reported he had discovered Paul in a room in the cellars of Herod's palace and had contacted the authorities there to allow them to bring him food and help.

After much discussion, it was decided most of the group from the west should return home as soon as possible to report news of Paul's situation. However, Lucas, Tychicus and Timothy insisted they would remain in Caesarea and be available to assist Paul in any way they could.

Philip and Zacchaeus agreed, and Theophilus offered the three of them to stay at his villa on the edge of the city. The others went to the port to try to secure passage west to either Corinth or Ephesus.

Zacchaeus had contacts everywhere it seemed; he pulled some strings and soon, he, Luke and Timothy were allowed to visit Paul. They found him bloodied and bruised in a dark cell in the bowels of the palace. He was relieved to see them.

"You have no idea how pleased I am to see you," said Paul, and then he promptly burst into tears. They gathered around him and held him. "I'm okay, really, I'm fine," he said. "I was just overwhelmed by it all."

"You don't look fine to me," said Lucas, "Timothy, help me get him into the light where I can see what needs to be done."

The next few days they managed to get him moved to a cell with a window where at least he could get air. Food, bedding, and clean clothes were brought, and Lucas cared for his wounds. Paul's body had endured so much physical hardship over the years, Lucas was amazed Paul had not suffered worse injury.

"I don't know how you are still alive, Paul, after all you have been through these last few years."

"Ouch!" winced Paul as Lucas began to examine him and tend the wounds on his face and back. "That really hurts."

Lucas gently pressed on Paul's side. "I think you have two broken ribs; they will take time to heal."

"I am alive because of the kindness of God. He obviously has things prepared in advance for me still to do."

He paused, winced again, then added,

"But I am also alive because of you, my dear beloved physician."

Over the next few days, all of Paul's friends who had travelled with him to Jerusalem came to visit and bade him farewell as they were soon to board a ship bound for Ephesus and then Corinth. There were tearful partings and Paul promised he would try to visit them again one day. They promised to send support as soon as they could. Paul asked Trophimus to return to Ephesus to continue copying the manuscripts of his letters and in the same way he asked Tychicus to remain with him in Caesarea for this purpose. Timothy wanted to stay longer, but Paul encouraged him also to return to Corinth and continue to visit the communities of believers around the Aegean. Paul asked Timothy to work closely with Titus and send news when they could. Of the original group, only Lucas and Tychicus stayed with him.

Five days after Paul arrived in Caesarea, news came from Jerusalem that the high priest Ananias was on his way to Caesarea, with some of the elders, accompanied by a Jewish lawyer called Tertullus. They had carefully agreed on their charges against Paul and were ready to present them to the governor, Felix.

CHAPTER II

Paul was summonsed and taken to the governor's residence where the hearing would take place. He was allowed to bring two supporters, so Lucas and Zacchaeus accompanied him.

Felix looked bored and slumped down in a chair on a dais. He had been governor of Judea for six years and was tired of the province and the continual conflicts he had with the Jewish authorities.

"Speak." Felix bellowed. "What do you want this time?"

Tertullus stepped forward and obsequiously bowed. Ananias initially refused to bow until a glare from Felix nudged him into a less than full bow. Tertullus straightened and began to present his case.

"We have enjoyed a long period of peace under you, and your foresight has brought about reforms in this nation. Everywhere and in every way, most excellent Felix, we acknowledge this with profound gratitude. But in order not to weary you further, I would request you be kind enough to hear us briefly."

Felix initially purred with satisfaction at the flattery, then barked at Tertullus.

"Get on with it, man, don't waste my time."

"We have found this man to be a troublemaker," Tertullus pointed at Paul, "stirring up riots among the Jews all over the world. He is a ringleader of the Nazarene sect and even tried to desecrate the temple, so we seized him."

Tertullus let these words sink in, then continued,

"By examining him yourself, you will be able to learn the truth about all these charges we are bringing against him."

The other Jews loudly joined in the accusations, asserting these

THE STORY OF PAUL III

things were true.

"Alright, alright, I get your point. Shut up all of you," shouted Felix over the din.

When it quietened down, he motioned for Paul to speak. Paul began by saying,

"I know that for several years you have been a judge over this nation, so I gladly make my defence. You can easily verify that no more than twelve days ago I went up to Jerusalem to worship. My accusers did not find me arguing with anyone at the temple or stirring up a crowd in the synagogues or anywhere else in the city. And they cannot prove to you the charges they are now making against me. However, I admit I worship the God of our ancestors as a follower of the Way, which they call a sect. I believe everything that is in accordance with the Law and is written in the Prophets, and I have the same hope in God as these men themselves have, of a resurrection of both the righteous and the wicked. So, I strive always to keep my conscience clear before God and man."

"Get on with it, I'm bored already," said Felix stifling a yawn.

"After an absence of several years, I came to Jerusalem to bring my people gifts for the poor and to present offerings. I was ceremonially clean when they found me in the temple courts doing this. There was no crowd with me, nor was I involved in any disturbance. But there are some Jews from the province of Asia, who ought to be here before you to bring charges if they have anything against me. Or these who are here should state what crime they found in me when I stood before the Sanhedrin, unless it was this one thing I shouted as I stood in their presence: 'It is concerning the resurrection of the dead that I am on trial before you today.'"

CHAPTER II

Well acquainted with the Way, Felix abruptly adjourned the proceedings.

"Alright, that will do. I've heard enough. When Commander Lysias comes," he said to Paul, "I will decide your case. Guards, take him back to his cell in Herod's palace. The rest of you get out of my sight and come back when you have all your witnesses ready."[14]

Felix grinned to himself as they shuffled disgruntledly out of the audience chamber. Felix knew Lysias would not be coming as he had already been sent off to Tiberius in Galilee to lick his wounds after his mishandling of the whole fiasco. *With luck*, he thought, *this man Paul will be forgotten by the Jewish council and in time made to pay to get himself out of confinement, and I will pocket the fee.* Felix was always eager to make money out of his position.

He ordered the centurion to keep Paul under guard. He did allow some freedom and permitted his friends to take care of his needs. Without these liberties, Paul undoubtedly would have died in prison.

As for Felix, so sure was he that nothing would happen, he left Caesarea to re-join his wife Drusilla who was staying at Herodium.

When this news reached the leaders of the believers in Caesarea, they knew Paul would have some respite but would not be free for a long while.

"Why has he gone to Herodium?" asked Lucas. Cornelius answered,

"King Herod the Great built himself a palace there about seventy years ago and modestly named it after himself. It's luxurious, with fabulous baths and gardens. The Roman Governors of Judaea requisitioned his former palace for their own residence after Herod died. I went there myself once when I was still an active officer. Felix

THE STORY OF PAUL III

married Drusilla, who is the great granddaughter of Herod, and she likes staying there as if she still owns the place. It's about sixty stadia from Jerusalem and a city has grown up around the palace to serve the governor."[15]

"It will be quite some time before we see Felix again by the sound of things," added Zacchaeus.

Sometime later, as expected, Felix came back to Caesarea with his wife Drusilla. He sent for Paul and listened to him speak about faith in Jesus. As Paul talked about righteousness, self-control, and the judgement to come, Felix was afraid.

"That's enough for now," he said. "You may leave. When I find it convenient, I will send for you."

Always looking for ways to line his pockets, Felix was a typical bureaucrat. He was hoping Paul would offer him a bribe to get himself released so he sent for him frequently and talked with him. Paul refused to pay a bribe, and soon Felix began to tire of talking to Paul.[16]

Lysias never came and Paul was not released.

The days of waiting turned into weeks and then months. No word was received from the leaders of the Jewish community or the authorities in Jerusalem. There was no sign of the Roman tribune Lysias, until finally Paul's nephew came with news. Paul was delighted to see him again.

"Jerusalem is a dangerous place these days, Uncle," said the young man. "The zealots are getting more active and there are continual attacks made on the Romans. Their methods of reprisal haven't changed much either. Crucifixions are almost a daily occurrence. Lysias virtually lost control of the city, and Felix removed him not

CHAPTER II

long after you were arrested and sent him to Tiberius in Galilee. He has been replaced by a stronger pair of hands. Every Zealot they had in prison was executed within days. Many people fear a full-scale insurrection."

Paul listened to his nephew and after a few moments continued

"How is your mother doing? Is she safe?"

"She is thinking about returning to Tarsus."

"Maybe that is for the best," said Paul.

∿∿∿

A week or so later, Lucas visited Paul bringing food.

While sharing the meal, Lucas said, "Paul, I have been thinking about my time here."

Paul looked quizzically at him. "I have been wondering what you have been doing. How is it going at Theophilus' house?"

"It is going well. Theophilus has set me up with my own scriptorium."

"A what?" asked Paul.

"Scriptorium," laughed Lucas. "Theophilus is an educated man and loves to show off his knowledge of Latin. It's a room set aside where I can write. He has also taken to calling me by the shortened Latin version of my name, Luke. I quite like it."

Paul grunted. "It will never catch on."

"What are you writing about?" asked Paul.

"Two things really. I have been hearing about the beginnings of the community of Jesus' followers in Jerusalem and here in Caesarea. I had a long talk with Philip who was one of the early leaders. Apparently, he went to Samaria and preached there. And he also met an Ethiopian official who had been in Jerusalem and obtained a copy of one of the Hebrew prophets, Isaiah. They met on a desert road, a long way south of here. It's a fascinating story."

"What really interests me," continued Lucas, "is how powerfully the Holy Spirit was involved right from the beginning. The Spirit seems to be so important."

"He is," said Paul.

"You call the Spirit 'he'," exclaimed Lucas. "Why do you do that?"

"Because he is the Spirit of the Father and of his Son Jesus. They, together with the Spirit, are the essence and nature of God. It's hard to understand if you try to work it out logically in your mind. Like all the things we see now, these things are perceived through the eyes of our hearts, not understood by our minds. We receive these things through revelation which is a gift from the Father to us, his beloved sons and daughters."

Lucas sat listening as Paul opened his heart to him.

"There is someone else you could talk to while you are here," said Paul. Lucas raised his eyebrows quizzically.

"You need to talk to Cornelius. He has a story to tell you. He was a Roman centurion many years ago here in Caesarea and met Peter who told him about Jesus. His conversion was unusual. Peter was telling him the good news and before he had the chance to say much, the Holy Spirit fell on everyone in the room." Paul chuckled as he related the story. "That's how it is with the Spirit; you never quite know what he will do next. Go and spend time with Cornelius,

CHAPTER II

he can tell you the whole story better than I can."

Their conversation spanned many events from the early years. Finally, Paul stopped and looked intently at Lucas.

"There is another story I want to tell you about, but it is hard for me to relay it."

"Oh?" said Lucas.

"Yes," Paul nodded. "It's my story."

"I have heard bits and pieces when you preached but never really sat and heard the story from the beginning. Do you want to tell me about it?"

"I think now is the right time," said Paul.

"Can I ask you some questions to fill in some gaps?" asked Lucas.

Paul nodded.

"When did your journey as a follower of Jesus begin?"

"As you know, I was born and raised in Tarsus. My family lived there, and my father was a tentmaker like me. It is where I learnt my trade. He was also a Pharisee."

"I didn't know there were Pharisees outside of Judea and Galilee," said Lucas.

"There are some, especially in the cities where there are large Jewish communities such as Alexandria. There were a few in my hometown, so naturally I wanted to become a Pharisee like my father. I was proud of being the son of a Pharisee. When I was a still a boy my father agreed to send me to Jerusalem to join the Pharisaical School of Gamaliel. My father knew many of the Jerusalem Pharisees personally and he arranged for me to live with one of the families."

"I studied under Gamaliel and was thoroughly trained in the law of our ancestors. I was zealous for God. I conformed strictly to all the rules of living as a Pharisee. I was extremely hard and the only way I could make it work was to suppress my own will and emotions and submit myself totally to the Law and how we thought it should be interpreted and lived. I became fanatical and critical of anyone who did not meet my standards. I think I must have been insufferable!

"I would succeed some of the time, but so often I failed and became depressed over my failures. When I began to feel better, I would try so much harder and become even more zealous thinking the Lord might be pleased with me if I tried harder. The truth was I never could, nor did I ever feel the approval of the Lord. Just his judgement. To deaden my pain, I was harder on my friends and fellow Pharisees. The more I judged them, the better I felt about myself. I would think, *At least I am better than them.* I lost quite a few friends in the process."

"Did you ever hear Jesus speak?" asked Lucas.

"No, sadly I didn't. But I did hear John the baptiser speak. He appeared out of nowhere it seems."

"When would that have been?" asked Lucas.

Paul paused and looked down as he tried to remember.

"It was over thirty years ago. Let me think… it was definitely the fifteenth year of the reign of Tiberius Caesar when Pontius Pilate was governor of Judea. Herod was the tetrarch of Galilee, his brother Philip tetrarch of Iturea and Traconitis, and Lysanias tetrarch of Abilene. I remember it was during the high priesthood of Annas and Caiaphas."

CHAPTER II

Lucas was astonished.

"How do you remember all those details, Paul?"

"Don't forget, I was a Pharisee. We are trained to remember things. We had to memorise the whole of the Torah in Hebrew before we qualified as a Pharisee, as if it makes any difference in the end."

"What do you mean?" asked Lucas.

"I have realised this religious behaviour leads to condemnation and guilt; it does not bring life. But I digress, back to John."

"I first heard about John when he started preaching down in the Jordan valley. News reached the High Priest and he sent some of us to hear what he was saying. Basically, to make sure he was not blaspheming."

"He was preaching a baptism of repentance for the forgiveness of sins and quoting words written in the book of Isaiah the prophet.

"Let me recite them to you in Greek as they were originally written in Hebrew. You can find them for yourself in the Septuagint, the Greek version, if you are really interested.

"A voice of one calling in the wilderness,

'Prepare the way for the Lord, make straight paths for him.

Every valley shall be filled in, every mountain and hill made low.

The crooked roads shall become straight, the rough ways smooth.

And all people will see God's salvation.'"

"There were crowds of people along the Jordan river. The day I was standing there among a group of us Pharisees, John looked straight at us. He said, 'You brood of vipers! Who warned you to flee from the coming wrath?'" Paul grinned and started to chuckle.[17]

"When I think of it now, it makes me laugh. At the time, we were deeply offended. But we were so full of our self-righteousness and self-importance in those days. John went on to say, 'Produce fruit in keeping with repentance. And do not say to yourselves, 'We have Abraham as our father.' For I tell you that out of these stones, God can raise up children for Abraham. The axe is already at the root of the trees, and every tree that does not produce good fruit will be cut down and thrown into the fire.' Well, that did it. His days were numbered. No one spoke to us, 'the Righteous ones,' like that."

Again, Paul laughed.

"I was furious. He dared to call us snakes, and he was probably absolutely right." Paul stopped talking for a while as his memory savoured the moment. Then he continued,

"People started calling out, 'What should we do then?' John answered, 'Anyone who has two shirts should share with the one who has none, and anyone who has food should do the same.' We even saw tax collectors coming to be baptized. They asked, 'Teacher, what should we do?'

"John replied, 'Don't collect any more than you are required to.' Some soldiers asked him, 'What about us? what should we do?'

He replied, 'Don't extort money and don't accuse people falsely; be content with your pay.' You know, Lucas. As I listened, I thought there was not much wrong with these answers. I was just offended he was disrespectful to us Pharisees."

"Who did people think he was?" asked Lucas.

"The people were hanging on his every word and were all

CHAPTER II

wondering if John might possibly be the Messiah. John seemed to know this, so he said, 'I baptize you with water. But one who is more powerful than I will come, the straps of whose sandals I am not worthy to untie. He will baptize you with the Holy Spirit and fire. His winnowing fork is in his hand to clear his threshing floor and to gather the wheat into his barn, but he will burn up the chaff with unquenchable fire.' Now I know what he was talking about, but back then I had no clue. My eyes were still blind, and I could not see the truth," said Paul.

"Where you there when he baptised Jesus? And did he go on preaching for long after this?" asked Lucas.

"No, I wasn't there when Jesus went to the Jordan, but I do know that not long after this John publicly rebuked Herod the tetrarch because of his marriage to Herodias, his brother's wife, and all the other evil things he had done. Herod had John arrested and locked up in prison. The rest is history as they say. He was beheaded sometime later."

"Did you ever hear Jesus teach?"

"No, I didn't. Part of my calling as a Pharisee required me to marry and family circumstances dictated I go back to Tarsus to find a suitable wife and get married. I left soon after for home. In the end, I was away from Jerusalem for more than two years. I did get married, but it wasn't a happy marriage. My wife didn't want to live in Jerusalem, and I didn't want to live in Tarsus. We had a child who died, and I don't think I knew how to handle her grief or my own. I was full of pain and anger and returned to Jerusalem alone."

There was a deep sadness in his voice as Paul recounted the story to Lucas. He continued,

"You don't need to add this to your story if you ever write it, Lucas, it's not important. But it helps explain why I was so obsessed and full of anger. It was my pain as much as anything driving me in those days.

"On my return to Jerusalem a couple of my relatives, Andronicus and Junia, who travelled from Rome for Passover came to stay with me. They arrived only a day or two after I returned from Tarsus, and we celebrated the Passover together. We three walked into the tumultuous events of the last week of Jesus' ministry. I arrived just before Passover and found out what had been going on in my absence. I had never heard the man Jesus speak but friends told me all about him. Literally the day following the Passover, some local friends woke me up, told me Jesus had been arrested and taken to the governor Pontius Pilate. I left my relatives and went to the city centre to find out what was happening.

"We got to the governor's palace just as Pilate came out to announce to the chief priests that he found no basis for a charge against the man Jesus. But they were all shouting and insisted, 'He stirs up the people all over Judea by his teaching. He started in Galilee and has come all the way here.'

"On hearing this, Pilate asked if the man was Galilean. When he learned Jesus was under Herod's jurisdiction, he sent him to Herod, who was also in Jerusalem at the time. So, we followed along with the crowd to see what would happen. When Herod saw Jesus, he was pleased. My friends told me Herod had been wanting to see Jesus for quite some time because he hoped to see him perform a miracle of some sort. Herod plied him with many questions, but Jesus refused to answer him. The chief priests and many of the teachers of the Law were standing there, vehemently accusing Jesus. We watched

CHAPTER II

Herod and his soldiers ridicule and mock him. They dressed him in a purple robe and sent him back to Pilate."

"Paul, I have never heard this part of the story before," said Lucas, "about being accused before Herod. I've got Mark's version of the trial, but he doesn't mention it at all."[18]

"Didn't you say Mark's account is strongly influenced by Simon Peter's memories of those awful days?" asked Paul. "Perhaps he didn't know about it. It is always the case; different people remember different things. I'm glad you are asking questions. It is so important the whole story is told. Keep on asking, Lucas. Write it down as you hear it and put it in your account. Who knows? Maybe someone will still be reading your story of Jesus' life in two thousand years' time if Jesus has not returned by then. What you are doing is of immense value, Lucas."

"I sincerely doubt it, Paul," replied Lucas. "When you wrote to your friends in Thessalonica, didn't you tell them he would come back suddenly from heaven with all those who have fallen asleep already? Then we who are alive will be taken up to join him. I'm sure it will be soon."

"Yes, I agree. But until it happens, people will need to read your account of Jesus' life. We don't know when he will return. In the meantime, let's get on with this. It is what the Father has given to you today, Lucas. My time here in Caesarea is a gift to you, to do this great work. Now, where was I? Are you ready for me to continue?"

Lucas nodded and picked up his stylus again. He dipped it into his ink and took a new sheet of parchment before looking expectantly at Paul.

"Eventually Jesus was handed over to be crucified. My friends were losing interest by this time, and we decided to go and get something to eat. Later in the day, we went out to watch the crucifixion. We took pleasure in sinners being punished. We laughed and said it would be a shame to waste a good crucifixion."

Paul stopped talking. His face clouded and he closed his eyes. His memories of the time were vivid and full of pain and shame. A tear gathered along his lower eyelid and fell down his cheek.

"Do you want to stop, Paul?" asked Lucas.

"No, I'm alright. Thank you." Paul waited a few minutes in silence, then said, "I was there. I saw him hanging on the cross. The blasphemer from Nazareth, we called him. Little did I know who he really was. I saw his naked body which had been ripped by lashes. I saw a crude crown of thorns jammed on his head. I heard his final cry. I watched him die. I know he died. I saw the nails tearing at his hands and feet. What a spectacle it was. I saw the blood. There was so much blood. I had never seen so much blood. Some of his family were there crying and in agony. I thought, '*now they know what losing a son feels like.*' In many ways, I was numb. I did not feel anything except my burning anger. It was getting dark, and I went back to my house as it was almost the Sabbath. I did not want to disobey God by breaking the Sabbath." Paul paused again, "The irony of it all.

"I thought it was the end of it," said Paul. "Little did I know it was just the beginning. Within days, stories emerged that Jesus had risen from the dead. I thought this was utterly ridiculous. I knew he was dead. I know I saw him die.

"Others will tell you about those early days in Jerusalem. If you get a chance to talk to Peter, he will help, others too. Philip here in Caesarea, he was one of the early followers. Have you talked to him yet?"

Lucas nodded.

"Let me tell you a bit more about my experience at that time," said Paul. "It must have been quite some time later before I personally got involved. By then the Nazarenes, or Followers of the Way as they preferred to call themselves, had grown in numbers in the city. Even a large number of priests became 'obedient to the faith' as they called it.

"I was continuing in my studies as a Pharisee and came up against them from time to time. I had become a member of a synagogue in Jerusalem called the Synagogue of the Freedmen made up of Jews from Cyrene and Alexandria as well as the provinces of Asia and Cilicia, my home area. One of our members, a man called Stephen became a follower of Jesus. He was such a wonderful young man. When I think of him now, he was a man full of God's grace and power. He performed great wonders and signs among the people. However, opposition arose from members of our synagogue. We argued with him, but we could not stand against the wisdom the Spirit gave him as he spoke.[19]

"We secretly persuaded some men to accuse him of blasphemy and report him to the priests. The usual accusations I get all the time now. 'We have heard Stephen speak blasphemous words against Moses and against God.' We stirred up the people and the elders and the teachers of the Law. They seized Stephen and brought him before the Sanhedrin. We produced false witnesses who testified, 'This fellow never stops speaking against this holy place and against the Law. For we have heard him say that this Jesus of Nazareth will destroy this place and change the customs Moses handed down to us.' All sorts of things like that.[20]

"He was dragged off and taken to the Council. Everyone sitting in the Sanhedrin looked intently at Stephen. He looked amazing. His face was like the face of an angel."

Paul recounted to Lucas everything Stephen said. Paul's razor-sharp forensic mind repeated Stephen's address to the Jewish authorities in astonishing detail. Lucas marvelled at the mind of Paul and his intellectual ability. He knew he was sitting in the presence of a colossus, perhaps one of the greatest minds the world had ever seen. In Lucas' opinion greater than Plato or Socrates. They worked together long into the afternoon as Lucas wrote, regularly stopping and questioning and checking a detail with 'the master' as he was now affectionately thinking of him.

"When the members of the Sanhedrin heard this, they were furious and were grinding their teeth." Paul paused, and then said, "Stephen, was full of the Holy Spirit. He looked up to heaven and saw the glory of God, and Jesus standing at the right hand of God. Then I heard him say, 'Look, I see heaven open and the Son of Man standing at the right hand of God.'

"This was too much for them, they covered their ears and yelling at the top of their voices, they rushed at him, dragged him out of the city to stone him. I went with the crowd and when we gathered outside the city wall, they laid their coats at my feet. While they were stoning him, Stephen prayed, 'Lord Jesus, receive my spirit.' Then he fell on his knees and cried out, 'Lord, do not hold this sin against them.' After he said this, a rock hit him right between his eyes. It was the fatal blow. He collapsed and died."[21]

There was another long pause as Paul again wiped his eyes.

CHAPTER II

Then he said,

"I approved of their killing of him.

"This was the beginning of a great persecution against the followers of Jesus in Jerusalem, and all except the apostles were scattered throughout Judea and Samaria. Godly men buried Stephen and mourned deeply for him. But I began to destroy them. I went from house to house; I dragged off men and women and put them in prison. I persecuted the followers of the Way to their deaths.

"I was totally convinced that I ought to do everything possible to oppose the name of Jesus of Nazareth. On the authority of the chief priests, I put many of the Lord's people in prison, and when they were put to death, I cast my vote against them. Many a time I went from one synagogue to another to have them punished, and I tried to force them to blaspheme. I was so obsessed with persecuting them that I even hunted them down in foreign cities."[22]

Paul's face showed the strain of these memories.

"I think you know what happened on one of those journeys. Don't you, Lucas? We can talk about it another time if you like. Now I need to rest."

"And I have much to sort out and think about," said Lucas. "Thank you, Paul. I know this wasn't easy."

∿∿∿

Lucas left Paul and went back to Theophilus' house. In his writing room, he collected the notes he had written and wrote down all he could remember of his conversation with Paul. The oil lamps Theophilus provided were beginning to sputter and smoke. Lucas rubbed his eyes, and then dozed off. He thought he was dreaming but knew he was suddenly very much awake. The room was dark, yet he felt a presence in the room. He had written about the Holy Spirit earlier, and he knew the presence of the Spirit was with him at that exact moment. There was a deep conviction growing within him. He was being given a specific twofold task by the Spirit. The first was to write an account of the things that happened among them, just as they were handed down by those who from the first were eyewitnesses of Jesus' life and servants of the word.

He sensed the Spirit urging him to carefully investigate everything himself from the beginning and to write an orderly account so people would know the certainty of the things they had been taught.[23]

As Lucas sat in the darkness, he was overwhelmed by the tangible presence of God's Spirit speaking to him. This was a new experience for him. He was sure the Spirit was speaking directly into his heart. It was as clear as an audible voice urging him to specifically write about all Jesus did and taught until the day he was taken up to heaven.

He also felt the Spirit was encouraging him to write down what happened after Jesus had ascended to heaven; to record what happened in Jerusalem in the following years. He felt the Spirit guiding him and instructing him to seek out Peter and hear his story. He was also to include Paul's story, but Paul's story was not finished yet. The last thing Lucas felt the Spirit impressing on him was to make the writing of the life of Jesus his priority while he was in Caesarea.

A light appeared in the doorway of the room. Theophilus held an oil lamp in his hand.

CHAPTER II

"Are you alright, Luke?" he asked as the pool of light cast by the lamp lit up Lucas' face. "Can I get you anything?"

"Theophilus, I'm fine, thank you. I have everything I need. In fact, it is clear to me what I have to do."

"Well, if there is anything I can do to help, just let me know. Why don't you go to bed? It will soon be dawn, and I suspect you have not slept much," he said gently.

Lucas stood and looked at his host.

"Thank you, most excellent Theophilus."

∿∿∿

The next morning, in his writing room, the 'scriptorium', Lucas sorted through the scrolls he had acquired. He quickly found the one he was looking for, the copy of Mark's life of Jesus. He had obtained it in Ephesus some time before. He carefully unrolled it and started to read. His finger moved along the lines and down the closely written columns as he read aloud the words John Mark had written. He re-read Mark's account of the trial of Jesus and saw there was no mention of Jesus before Herod.

He decided to follow Mark's account and add the new information he was hearing. He thought if he ever encountered Mark again he would tell him what he was doing and what a help his version was to him.

A servant brought him a basket of freshly made barley rolls and a dish of crushed olives and garlic. Lucas broke open the rolls and spread them with the mixture of crushed olives and garlic realising how hungry he was. The morning turned into afternoon and again a servant came and stood in front of Lucas.

"Yes? What is it?" asked Lucas.

"The master asked me to tell you he has prepared food for you and requests you join him. He has a guest with him who he thinks you will be interested to meet."

The servant, realising he had said too much, quickly withdrew. Lucas wondered who the guest was as he placed a marker in the scroll.

Lucas left the scriptorium and walked across the light filled atrium. The sun shone into the room through the roof opening above illuminating a fountain in the pool which collected rainwater in the centre of the atrium. He could hear voices coming from the triclinium and then laughter. Lucas approached the door. Theophilus stood from the couch and invited Lucas to recline on his left. On the other couch reclined Cornelius who Lucas knew was one of the leaders in the community of followers of Jesus in Caesarea.

"You have met Luke I believe?" Theophilus asked Cornelius.

"Well, we have met but we have not had an opportunity to talk," said Cornelius as he stood to greet Paul. "I am delighted to meet you properly at last."

Lucas clasped Cornelius' arm in the Roman way and the two men smiled at each other. They both sat and stretched out on the couches at the table. Servants entered carrying several platters of food and placed them in front of the three of them.

"Friends, we thank God our Father for providing us with this food from his bounty and for sending his son to reveal him to us and bring us home to him as his sons," said Theophilus.

CHAPTER II

"Now let us eat. I have taken the liberty of preparing Gentile food today as none of our Jewish brothers are with us. I wouldn't want to offend them. However, as it is just us, let us enjoy some flavours of home."

The two men nodded and smiled as they looked at the spread in front of them. The centrepiece was a roasted suckling pig covered in apple and orange slices. Freshly caught grilled mullet surrounded by various local vegetables and beans and a platter of fresh oysters and slices of lemon were placed nearby. These delights were accompanied by a bowl of pungent garum sauce, while fresh figs and new season grapes cascaded out of a silver bowl. It had been a long time since Lucas tasted such food.

"I have been eager to meet you, Cornelius," said Lucas. "My dear friend Paul has told me a little about you."

Cornelius nodded amicably and this encouraged Lucas to continue,

"Paul suggested I ask you about how you became a follower of Jesus."

"Luke is writing down the stories of how it all began," explained Theophilus.

"I would happily tell you," said Cornelius. "My life has never been the same since."

"Let us eat first," said Theophilus, "then you can go and get your pens and parchment, Luke. It would be a shame to let the food get cold."

They all agreed and soon their plates were filled with ample servings of food. The wine was a rich vintage from Judea that perfectly accompanied the meal. After eating and chatting together, Cornelius finally smacked his lips and wiped his greasy chin with a linen napkin.

"So, shall I begin?" he said. Lucas nodded and rolled over to pick up his pen the servant had brought to him.

"I was a centurion back then, stationed here in Caesarea, in charge of a section known as the Italian Cohort. This must have been nearly twenty-five years ago. My family and I were devout and God-fearing people. I was tired of the empty religion of Rome. When we came here to Judea, I started to pray to the Jewish God."

"You were generous to the poor too. I remember," said Theophilus.

"One day, at about three in the afternoon, I was praying and had a vision. I distinctly saw an angel of God come to me and call me by my name. I was astonished because I had never had an experience like that before.

"The truth is, I was terrified, and I asked, 'What is it, my Lord?' The angel said to me my prayers and gifts to the poor have come up as a memorial offering before God. He told me to send men to Joppa to bring back a man named Simon who is called Peter."

"Do you mean *the* Simon Peter?" asked Lucas.

"Yes, exactly. The angel said he was staying with Simon, a tanner, whose house was by the sea in Joppa. Then the angel disappeared, as suddenly as he had come."

"What did you do then?" asked Lucas.

"I called two of my servants and one of my soldiers, who was also a God fearer, and told them everything that had just happened and sent them to Joppa to find Peter.

CHAPTER II

"I have since found out from Peter that about noon the same day, as my men were on their way and approaching the city, Peter had gone up on the roof to pray. He was hungry and wanted something to eat, and while the meal was being prepared, he fell into some sort of a trance. He told me later he saw heaven open and something like a large sheet being let down to earth by its four corners. It contained all kinds of four-footed animals, as well as reptiles and birds, everything unclean for Jews to eat. He says he heard a voice telling him to get up, kill and eat.

"He was shocked and said, 'Surely not, Lord! I have never eaten anything impure or unclean.' Peter then told me the voice spoke to him a second time saying, 'Do not call anything impure that God has made clean.'

"Apparently this happened three times. Then the sheet was taken back to heaven."

"What did Peter understand this to mean?" asked Lucas.

"Peter says while he was wondering about the meaning of the vision, the men I sent arrived at the tanner's house and stopped at the gate. They called out, asking if Simon who was known as Peter was staying there.

"Peter says the Spirit said to him, "Simon, three men are looking for you. Get up and go downstairs. Do not hesitate to go with them, for I have sent them.

"When Peter went down, he said to the men, "I'm the one you're looking for. Why have you come?"

"This is an amazing story," said Lucas. "What did the men say?"

"They said they had been sent by me, a Roman centurion; that I was a righteous and God-fearing man, who was respected by all the Jewish people. They then told him how an angel had instructed me to ask for a man called Simon Peter to come to my house so that I could hear what he had to say. To their absolute amazement, Peter invited these Gentile men into the house to be his guests and they ended up staying the night.

"The next day, Peter, and some of the believers from Joppa, set out with them. I was expecting them, and I had called together my relatives and close friends so they could meet him too. As soon as Peter arrived and entered my house, I was overwhelmed and fell at his feet in reverence. But Peter made me get up. 'Stand up,' he said, 'I am only a man myself.' He was humble and ordinary.

"I brought him inside to meet my family and friends; it was quite a large gathering of people. He said to us: 'You are well aware that it is against our law for a Jew to associate with or visit a Gentile. But God has shown me I should not call anyone impure or unclean. So, when I was sent for, I came without raising any objection. May I ask why you sent for me?"

"Did you tell him about your vision?" asked Lucas.

"I told Peter exactly what I have just told you." Cornelius answered.

"He listened carefully to what I said, then Peter started to speak. I'll never forget what he said.

"He told us God does not show favouritism but accepts from every nation those who fear him and do what is right. He told us God sent to the people of Israel, the good news of peace through Jesus Christ, who is Lord of all. Peter told us what happened throughout the province of Judea, beginning in Galilee after the baptism that John preached, and how God anointed Jesus of Nazareth with the

CHAPTER II

Holy Spirit and power. He said Jesus went around doing good and healing all who were under the power of the devil because God was with him."

"Had you heard about Jesus before, Cornelius?" asked Lucas.

"I had heard many stories and reports about Jesus. Peter said they were witnesses of everything Jesus did in the country of the Jews and in Jerusalem. How the troops in Jerusalem had killed him by hanging him on a cross. I had heard about this too. Then he said God raised him from the dead on the third day and he was seen by numerous people. These were the witnesses whom God had already chosen. He meant himself and his friends who ate and drank with Jesus after he rose from the dead.

"Peter said Jesus commanded them to preach to the people and to testify he is the one whom God appointed as judge of the living and the dead. Then he said all the Jewish prophets had testified about him and everyone who believed in him would receive forgiveness of sins through his name. That is the gist of what he said. It was more detailed at the time, but it was many years ago now. What happened next though, I will never forget."

Lucas put his pen down and looked intently at Cornelius. There was a curious look on his face, and he seemed to tremble slightly as if experiencing something special.

"As Peter was still speaking, something amazing happened to all of us. I know now it was the Holy Spirit who came upon us all. We began to laugh and cry and started to speak in strange, heavenly languages and we were all praising God."

A tear formed in Cornelius' eye and slowly rolled down his cheek. He wiped it with the back of his hand and sniffed loudly.

"The Jewish believers who had come with Peter were astonished. The gift of the Holy Spirit had been poured out even on us Gentiles."

Cornelius chuckled to himself as he recounted the story.

"Then Peter said, 'Surely no one can stand in the way of their being baptized with water. They have received the Holy Spirit just as we have.' So, they baptized us in the name of Jesus Christ. It was a day to remember. My life has never been the same since."

Lucas sat in silence listening to Cornelius retell the story. He had stopped writing notes some time before and knew he would need to hear it again. Lucas and Theophilus did not speak when Cornelius finished his story. They lay back on their couches lost in thought. Finally, Theophilus said.

"More wine anyone?"[24]

∿∿∿

After a few days, Lucas went back to see Paul in Herod Agrippa's palace. There was still no word from Jerusalem. Felix had not been in Caesarea for weeks. Sometimes, Paul wondered if he had been forgotten. When Lucas arrived, Paul was pleased to see him. Lucas wanted to check out his recent injuries and see how his broken ribs were repairing.

After a thorough check, Lucas told Paul he was pleased with his recovery. He was getting stronger each day. The rest was obviously doing him good.

"Paul, I want to tell you how I am getting on with my writing. Up to now, I have been making notes about what happened in the days following the resurrection. I have been talking with you and

CHAPTER II

Cornelius, as you suggested, and also Philip. But the Holy Spirit has spoken to me about my writing."

"Really? That is interesting to hear. What is he saying to you?"

"He told me to concentrate on Jesus' life and ministry first, especially while we are here in Judea."

Paul looked interested and encouraged him to continue.

"Go on," he said.

"You know I have a copy of the manuscript John Mark wrote about the life of Jesus. I have been reading it and making notes. I keep picking up stories he has not mentioned, and I have been looking at where they fit in the story. I have been thinking I would like to try to meet some of the people he mentions and find out more about those days. Almost thirty years has passed since Jesus returned to the Father and many of the people who knew him and met him have died already. I want to write down the stories of those still alive before they pass on too."

"This is an excellent idea, Lucas. You could start here in Caesarea. You know Zacchaeus met Jesus?" said Paul.

"I do. In fact, I have written his story down already. I love the bit about him being up a tree. I can just imagine it. We've had lots of talks together and he has given me some suggestions about people I should talk to. He mentioned two sisters in Bethany who were close friends of Jesus. I hear one of them is an excellent cook.

"That sounds like it would be a productive use of your time. You could travel around, even go up to Galilee. You should meet up with James in Jerusalem. He will be able to introduce you to many people. He knows everybody. I don't think there are any of the original disciples still in Judea or Galilee. They have taken this good news all over the world. But occasionally they come back, especially Peter and John, as his mother is still in Capernaum. Galilee would not be far away. If things change here and I need you to come back, I could send for you." Paul was enthusiastically warming to Lucas' idea.

"Now, one other thing," continued Paul. "I have been meaning to tell you this for quite some time."

Lucas looked at him with interest.

"When I was being held at the Antonia Fortress in Jerusalem, I had the chance to talk with the commander of the garrison. His name is Claudius Lysias."

Lucas' eyes widened at the mention of the commander's name.

"Did you say his name was Claudius Lysias?"

"I did," said Paul. "He said he knows you. He said he grew up in Philippi, and this is the best bit. He told me his aunt is none other than Lydia."

"This is extraordinary. Of course, I know him. He was a friend of mine from my youth, but I haven't seen him or heard of him for years, not since he joined the army."

"My nephew says Lysias has been posted to head the Roman garrison in Tiberius up in Galilee. Maybe if you go to Galilee, he might be willing to meet you."

∿∿∿

Lucas collected sheets of papyrus so he could write down the things he heard from any eyewitnesses he might meet. A few days later, he visited Paul again. This time he came with Tychicus and Zacchaeus.

CHAPTER II

"Are you off soon, Lucas?" asked Paul.

"Yes, in a few days. I am going to Jerusalem first. Zacchaeus is coming with me to show me around and we are going to see who we can find there. He is going to take me to several of the places where Jesus taught and things happened."

Paul turned to Zacchaeus looking steadily into his eyes.

"Will you take him to where *it* happened?"

Zacchaeus paused, looked at Lucas, then said to Paul,

"Yes, to Skull Hill. It is a dreadful place. It has been for years. An endless succession of crucifixions. There must have been thousands there since *the one* all those years ago."

There was a long silence in the room until Tychicus broke it.

"What about the garden on the Mount of Olives, Gethsemane?" he asked. "Isn't that where the tomb was?"

"No," replied Zacchaeus. "The tomb was close to Skull Hill, not up on the Mount of Olives."

"However, I still think it would be good to go to the Mount of Olives and also to the garden at Skull Hill," added Lucas.

"The tomb is still there," said Zacchaeus. "But of course, it is where Joseph of Arimathea's is buried now. It was his tomb in the first place. There is nothing to see now except Joseph's tomb."

"Indeed," said Paul. "As for Jesus, he is not there. He is risen. I am sure it would be interesting to visit these sites, but we are not worshipping a dead martyr but the risen Son of God. We are in him and he is in us. There is no value in visiting places where he once was as if he is some historical relic. His presence is not there, it is here." Paul placed his hand on his chest and gently tapped it. "He is living here and we are in him. He is always with us."

After more discussion, Paul turned to Tychicus and asked about the copying of the parchments he had been doing.

"We have a small collection of them now, Paul. They are all copies of the originals you have written. Do you want a list?"

Paul nodded.

"Well, there is your first one you wrote to the brothers in Galatia, then the two you wrote to Thessalonica, one to the Philippian community, the Colossian letter and your personal one to Philemon. Do you want it included?"

Paul nodded again as he listened.

Tychicus continued,

"Then there are at least two of the four letters you wrote to Corinth. There are a couple of them which have gone missing, but I hope I can track them down next time I am in Corinth. Then, of course, there is the last one you sent to Rome. Are you going to write anymore, Paul?"

"I don't know. If the situation demands it, I might. I have been thinking while I have time here waiting in Caesarea to maybe write a more general letter to our friends in Asia and Ephesus. But nothing is pressing just yet."

CHAPTER III

As soon as Lucas and Zacchaeus arrived in Jerusalem, they went straight to Mnason's house. Lucas had stayed at his house some months before when Paul first arrived back in the city. Mnason was a Jew, originally from Cyprus, and familiar with the ways of Greeks, which made Lucas feel comfortable. Mnason welcomed them warmly and was eager to hear news of Paul in Caesarea.

The next day, they contacted the leaders of the Followers of the Way in the city. James, who was a half-brother of Jesus and the main leader of the group, politely welcomed them. After seating them and serving them wine and almonds, he asked how Paul was.

"Is there anything he needs? How is he physically? He disappeared so suddenly after his arrest we didn't know where he was."

Lucas was about to tell him about Paul's situation when James continued,

"I suspect he wants to know what we did with the money he brought from the brothers in Macedonia and those other places. I don't remember which places. Have you come here to find out?"

"No," said Lucas. "I'm here because I wanted to know more about Jesus and how this all began."

"Oh, I see," said James, looking visibly more relaxed. "Please stay and break bread with me. I'm interested to hear more of your plan."

James called for a servant to bring more wine and prepare food for them. Soon, they were sitting together chatting, eating, and sharing news. Lucas was able to report on Paul's condition which seemed to reassure him. James was interested in Lucas' desire to investigate the beginnings of the community of believers. He listened intently as Lucas shared his thoughts. Finally, he spoke.

"I like your plan. I want to help you in any way I can. I have been thinking about these things lately. My brother appeared to me alive after his crucifixion. On several occasions he said he would return to us. We have been waiting and longing for this to happen. But it is over thirty years ago now. We have relied on the memories of those who knew him to remind us of his words but of course everyone is getting older. Many have died and some… well, you know how it is with the elderly, the stories tend to get a bit hazy and for some they tend to become… How shall I put it? Embroidered in the telling."

They all laughed, and Zacchaeus grinned. "I have no idea what you are talking about. The tree I climbed was the tallest in Jericho."

"My point exactly," said James. "However, joking aside, there is someone you need to meet."

"Who's that?" asked Lucas.

"My mother, Mary," answered James. "Although quite old, she is still in Galilee. She lives with her sister, my aunt Salome, at John's house in Capernaum. John comes to visit them whenever he is back in the country, which is few these days. I am sure she would welcome a visit."

This news encouraged Lucas.

CHAPTER III

James spoke again.

"There are people here in the city we can introduce you to but give us time before we take you to them. My suggestion would be to go to Galilee first. As I said, my mother is getting older. Perhaps I will come with you, and it will give me some time with her too. She might need someone to nudge her if her memory becomes a little shaky. How does this sound, Lucas?"

"I would be delighted for you to accompany me. You know the route and the area having grown up there. I think it's an excellent idea."

"In which case," added Zacchaeus, "I will stay here in Judea and Jerusalem and join you when you return. But first, I have received a message from a friend in Bethany and an invitation for dinner. Are you interested?"

"Who is it from?" asked Lucas.

"The best cook in Judea," laughed Zacchaeus. "My dear friend Martha. She lives alone now. Both her sister Mary and brother Lazarus died some years ago. But she still knows how to cook a meal as she will not only demonstrate but tell you. She has a story to tell you about a visit from Jesus."

"I am intrigued," said Lucas.

"Oh, I know you won't be disappointed." added James "Just pray she serves her version of stuffed vine leaves. Her pigeon and olive dish is glorious. Can I come, Zacchaeus?"

Both men were enthusiastic discussing Martha's culinary creations.

Two days later, after having visited Martha, Lucas and Zacchaeus were back at Mnason's house.

With the memory of the amazing meal still in the forefront of his mind, Lucas pondered the things he heard and what they discussed at Martha's home. He took out the parchment and looked again at the notes he had written. He turned to James.

"Something Martha said surprised me." Lucas searched his notes.

"She told me about the time Jesus was at their home for a meal. She had been busy preparing the meal and fretting about getting everything prepared as there were thirteen extra mouths to feed with Jesus and his twelve hungry, young disciples. She said she walked into the room where Jesus was with them all and found her sister Mary sitting at Jesus' feet listening to him. Martha said she got angry and walked up to Jesus demanding he instruct her sister to help her with the cooking. I carefully noted what she said."

Lucas found the section in his notes.

"She told me Jesus said to her, 'Martha, Martha, you are worried and upset about many things, but few things are needed or indeed only one. Mary has chosen what is better, and it will not be taken away from her.' This sounds harsh to me. It is not how I imagined he was like. But Martha insisted this is what Jesus said. She made me read it back to her to make sure I had it written correctly."[25]

"The problem you Gentiles have is you do not understand us, Jews, or our ways," answered James. "It has always been like this ever since Paul started preaching to the Gentiles and Greeks. We, Jews, are different; our customs are different. Our ways of speaking are different. The fact the good news has come to the non-Jewish people of the world is indeed wonderful, as Paul so rightly reminds us. But it comes with, how shall I put it…communication difficulties."

Lucas looked at him. "Explain please, help me understand."

CHAPTER III

"Well," said James, "to your Gentile ears, it sounds like Jesus is reprimanding her. It was in fact the opposite. Did you notice Jesus said her name twice?"

Lucas nodded.

"I asked her about it. She was emphatic. Martha said he spoke her name twice and when she told me this, she looked… Well, how shall I say it? She looked serene, almost joyful."

"Exactly," said James. "You see, Lucas, when we, Jews, say someone's name twice in this way, it is a sign of great affection. Martha did not feel rebuked, she felt loved by him. He often said this; he even said it over Jerusalem once."

Lucas stood up.

"Of course! Now it all makes sense. I didn't realise it at the time."

"What are you talking about?" asked James.

"It's what Jesus said to Paul the day he met him on the Damascus road. Paul was known as Saul then. Paul told me and now, when I think about it, he had the same look as Martha did. When Jesus spoke to Paul, he said, 'Saul, Saul, why are you persecuting me?' He loved him! Even as a persecutor of his followers."

"Jesus said that to Saul?" James had an astonished look on his face. "I didn't know that. I am so surprised. The things I hear about my brother never cease to amaze me. I do wish I had taken more notice of him before he died."

The next day, James and Lucas set off for Galilee. As they walked the road north through the region of Samaria, James recounted to Lucas many of the stories Jesus had told during his short period of activity. There were a few stories Lucas had never heard and he was eager to write them down. They would stop while he painstakingly wrote them on his sheets of papyrus. Consequently, the journey was slow but neither seemed concerned. James had become eager to ensure Lucas got the details as accurately as possible. One day they passed close to one of Herod's country residences.

"Jesus called him a fox," said James.

"Why was that?" asked Lucas.

"Some of the Galilean Pharisees were more sympathetic to Jesus than the Jerusalem ones. On one occasion, they came to him and told to him to leave and go somewhere else because Herod wanted to kill him. Jesus laughed and said, 'Go tell that fox I will keep on driving out demons and healing people today and tomorrow, and on the third day, I will reach my goal. In any case, I must press on today and tomorrow and the next day, for surely no prophet can die outside Jerusalem.'

"He then said those words I told you about before," said James.

'Jerusalem, Jerusalem, you who kill the prophets and stone those sent to you, how often I have longed to gather your children together, as a hen gathers her chicks under her wings, and you were not willing. Look, your house is left to you desolate. I tell you, you will not see me again until you say, 'Blessed is he who comes in the name of the Lord.'"[26]

The two men sat staring across the landscape in front of them. Then Lucas carefully wrote the words down.

∿∿∿

The next day's journey took them through a small town called

CHAPTER III

Nain. James told Lucas what happened there when Jesus visited. He said large crowds followed wherever Jesus and his disciples went, and as they were approaching the town gate, a dead person was being carried out for burial.

"The dead man was the mother's only son, and she was a widow. A large crowd from the town was with her. When Jesus saw her, his heart went out to her. Jesus told the woman, 'Don't cry.'

"Then he went up and touched the bier they were carrying the dead man on, and the bearers stood still. Jesus said, 'Young man, I say to you, get up!' The dead man sat up and began to talk, and Jesus gave him back to his mother," said James.[27]

"They were all filled with awe and praised God saying, 'A great prophet has appeared among us. God has come to help his people.' The news spread throughout Judea and the surrounding country. Everyone one was talking about it. The last I heard, the boy is still alive. He became a follower of Jesus and is living somewhere down in Alexandria."

James carried on talking about those early days.

"There was a real transition in those brief years. Jesus spent quite a bit of time in Galilee and people who knew him often sat and talked with him, invited him for meals and were not particularly aggressive towards him, except at home. However, things were different in Judea and in Jerusalem, of course."

Lucas stopped writing and turned to James. "What do you mean 'except at home'?"

"You know we all grew up in Nazareth, don't you? Even though he was born down south in Bethlehem, we grew up in Nazareth. Jesus was the oldest, then I was born next. I was actually born in

Egypt. We moved back to Nazareth after King Herod died, when it was safe. Obviously, we just thought Jesus was like us; we didn't realise who he really was. In fact, I was not convinced even when he began his teaching ministry. Sibling stuff, you know?

"I remember when Jesus went off for a couple of months down to Judea to seek out our relative John the baptizer. He must have been about thirty by then. My father had died some years before and we all carried on with the family carpentry business at home, but I felt quite annoyed Jesus had wandered off like that. He left me to get on with everything. My mother told me to leave it and said we would know when his time had come. Whatever she meant by that, I had no idea.

"Jesus turned up a few weeks later and didn't come home as we thought he would. Instead, he went down to the lake, to Capernaum and by all accounts started preaching there. I know this because he visited my uncle and aunt, Zebedee and Salome and our cousins, James and John. The next thing we heard, those two boys had left their family fishing business and started to act as his disciples. There were wild rumours circulating about some miraculous healings being attributed to him, and the whole family was talking about it.

"After a while, Jesus came back to Nazareth. He stayed for a few days then on the Sabbath day, he went to the synagogue as he always did. As usual, we were all there. I remember it clearly. He was sitting next to me. Suddenly, he stood up to read, and the scroll of the prophet Isaiah was handed to him. Unrolling it, he found the place where it is written:

'The Spirit of the Lord is on me, because he has anointed me to proclaim good news to the poor. He has sent me to proclaim freedom for the prisoners and recovery of sight for the blind, to set

CHAPTER III

the oppressed free, to proclaim the year of the Lord's favour.'"

James sat staring into the distance.

"I remember it as if it was yesterday. He rolled up the scroll, gave it back to the attendant and sat down. The eyes of everyone in the synagogue were staring at him. Suddenly, he said, 'Today this scripture is fulfilled in your hearing.'

"Well, you could hear a pin drop. People started murmuring and whispering. Initially, they spoke well of him and were amazed at the gracious words coming from his lips. I could hear people saying, 'Isn't this Joseph's son?'

"Then, it went quiet, and Jesus said to everyone, 'Surely you will quote this proverb to me: 'Physician, heal yourself!' And you will tell me, 'Do here in your hometown what we have heard that you did in Capernaum.' Truly I tell you, no prophet is accepted in his hometown. I assure you that there were many widows in Israel in Elijah's time when the sky was shut for three and a half years and there was a severe famine throughout the land. Yet Elijah was not sent to any of them, but to a widow in Zarephath in the region of Sidon. And there were many in Israel with leprosy in the time of Elisha the prophet, yet not one of them was cleansed, only Naaman the Syrian.'

"It was shocking. I felt so embarrassed sitting there next to him with everyone glaring at him. They were incredibly angry. The people were furious when they heard this. They jumped up, grabbed him, and dragged him out of the synagogue. I was convinced they would demand the thirty-nine lashes. Instead, they drove him out of the town, and took him to the brow of the hill on which the town was built to throw him off the cliff. I was sure he would be killed. But he just walked right through the crowd and left town."²⁸

James stopped talking and watched Lucas write.

"I had no idea back then what he was talking about. It's much clearer to me now."

A few days later, James and Lucas crossed the Jezreel valley and headed up into Galilee towards Nazareth. James took Lucas to the old family home and carpenter's shop now run by the son of his youngest brother Jude. Jude was one of the main leaders of the Followers of Jesus within Galilee. James was eager for Lucas to meet him and hear his memories of his older brother. There was great excitement at their arrival and soon various family members and relatives came to greet James and his companion.²⁹

They ended up staying for a while as Lucas collected more material for his book. Lucas asked to visit the synagogue, but James suggested he would not be welcome as he was a Gentile.

"I could go," said James, "I thought you might be interested in seeing our family line through our father Joseph. I can go and get it and bring it out, as long as I take it back."

Lucas was interested and James went off to talk to the rabbi. He came back an hour later with a scroll. They sat down and unrolled it. Lucas had never seen anything like it before. It went back thirty-seven generations right to the time of Adam. As Lucas read out the names, he got to the final one.

"The son of Seth, the son of Adam." Then, he added a final one, "the son of God!"

"I never thought of it like that," gasped James. "It's true, the son of God! Lucas, you must write it down. I can help you. It has to go

CHAPTER III

in your account. We, Jews, so value our heritage. We don't record the family line of our mothers, but we really value the father's line. Even though my father was not Jesus' father, our family line is through Joseph, who is a descendant of King David, the tribe of Judah, right back to Adam."[30]

After a week or so, James and Lucas decided to go on to Capernaum as news had come that Mary would be happy to meet Lucas. It was an easy walk to Capernaum and James took Lucas via the town of Tiberius on the southern shore of the lake.

"This place doesn't feel Jewish," said Lucas as they walked through the streets.

"It isn't," said James. "There was hardly anything here until about forty years ago. But Herod decided he liked the hot springs in the area and started to build a complex around the springs. Before long, a whole town was built and populated with Gentiles. It's become quite big now.'

"Look up there on the hill," James pointed at a villa on the town. "Do you see the large building? It was a villa Herod Antipas built for himself. When he died, about fifteen years ago, the Romans requisitioned it and installed a procurator there to rule the whole province of Galilee. There was a new one appointed recently. I don't know anything about him, but I think he used to be the commander of the garrison at the Antonia Fortress in Jerusalem."

"Yes, I know," said Lucas. "His name is Claudius Lysias."

James stopped. Looking surprised, he asked.

"How do you know this?"

"It's a rather long story," replied Lucas. "Lysias was the officer who rescued Paul from the mob in the temple and sent him down to Caesarea. But Paul talked with Lysias before he went to Caesarea. He is a Greek, not a Roman, and he grew up in Philippi, my hometown."

"What?" exclaimed James. "Don't tell me, you know him."

"More than that," laughed Lucas. "We were friends when we were young. He went off to Rome and joined the army. I stayed in Philippi and became a doctor. But more to the point, he is the nephew of Lydia, one of the leaders of the believers in Philippi."

"How amazing! This can't be coincidental," said James. "This must be for a purpose. Do you want to go and meet him?"

"Yes, I think I do. I think this is something Father wants me to do."

James and Lucas stayed the night with believers in Tiberius, and the next day, having talked again about Lysias, they decided Lucas would go alone to the villa and seek an audience. James accompanied him through the streets to the villa. It had been fortified in recent years and there were guards at the heavy wooden gate.

Lucas walked up to the guard who looked at him with a surly scowl.

"What do you want?" the guard demanded.

"I request an audience with his excellency the Procurator, the Tribune Claudius Lysias," said Lucas.

"Why would he want to see you?" replied the guard.

"I am Antonius Lucas, a physician of the illustrious city of Philippi and I bring news of his aunt, the Lady Claudia Lydia of Philippi," said Lucas, "and the procurator will not want me to be kept waiting. Now get moving before I report you." Lucas was

CHAPTER III

surprised by his assertiveness.

The guard appeared anxious and told Lucas to wait while he disappeared through a doorway in the gate. In a few minutes, Lucas heard raised voices coming from within and suddenly the gate opened and out ran Lysias followed by the flustered guard and a servant.

"Lucas! Lucas, is it really you? My dear friend!"

Lysias approached Lucas and clasped his forearm in the Roman fashion and then to the surprise of everyone threw his arms around him. Lysias quickly recovered and turned and cuffed the guard and demanded he get back on duty. With that, he again put his arm around Lucas' shoulder and led him inside the official residence.

The two men spent all afternoon talking about the past and sharing news of friends and family back home in Philippi. The sun began to set, and evening drew on. Finally, Lucas started to leave.

"Will we meet again?" asked Lysias.

"I hope so," said Lucas. "As long as my friend Paul is held in Caesarea, I am staying in the province collecting material for the account of the life of Jesus. I will come again if I can."

"I doubt I will be in Caesarea in the near future. Felix doesn't want me going near your man Paul for some reason. In fact, I have applied to leave the province altogether. I am hoping to return to Rome. If I can, I will go via Philippi and see my family. I am more than a little intrigued about what you have told me about my aunt Lydia."

"Let's not lose contact again, my friend," said Lucas. "If ever Paul gets sent to Rome, as he wants, I will probably go with him. I would like to find you there if that happens."

"I'll find a way to send word to you if I get there," said Lysias as they came to the gate of the fortified residence.

Before parting, they clasped their forearms together, and then Lucas walked off into the night.

The next day, James and Lucas left Tiberius and followed the lake road north through Magdala and Gennesaret. They arrived in Capernaum at the top of the lake after a four hour walk. The lake was on their right throughout their walk. Fishing boats dotted the water as fishermen worked their trade. From time-to-time, James, well known in the area, waved to men who recognised him.

They entered the town of Capernaum and passed along its narrow streets as people stopped to greet James. He introduced Lucas to many of them and soon word spread of James' visit with a Greek follower of Jesus. Eventually, they were standing at the door of the home of James' aunt, Salome. Her husband, Zebedee had died many years before and she now lived with her older sister Mary in the house belonging to Salome's son, John, the former fisherman and one of the most important leaders among the followers of Jesus.

Salome greeted them warmly.

"How is mother?" asked James.

"She is well and excited you are here to visit her. She is particularly looking forward to meeting this handsome Greek. Come through, she is out the back in the courtyard. She doesn't do well in this dreadful heat we've been having."

They came out of the stuffy darkness of the house into a bright courtyard where a colourful awning was spread across one side. There, sat Mary the mother of Jesus. James walked over to her and bent down to kiss her on her forehead.

CHAPTER III

"So good to see you, Imi. You are looking well."

"James, my son, I am so glad to see you. It's been far too long."

"It has been busy down in Jerusalem. I'm sorry I haven't been up to see you lately."

"That's what you always say. It's been over a year, you know. One day I'll be gone, and then you will wish you had been more often. Anyway, you are here now and it's all that matters. Now, is this the Greek?"

Lucas approached, dropped to his knees, and bowed.

"Oh! Enough of the bowing. I'm just an old woman, you know. Stand up, let me look at you. Yes, they were right. You are handsome."

Lucas stood and looked at the tiny woman sitting on a pile of cushions in front of him. His heart was racing, and he found tears welling up in his eyes.

"You are the mother of my Lord!" he exclaimed.

"Yes, yes, yes, but he's my lord too and I just happen to be his mother. There's nothing special about me. Come on, sit down here next to me, Lucas, and let's have a lovely talk. Salome, get some refreshments for these weary travellers, please. And, James, while you are here there are some things we need you to do. There is a broken latch on the door. It needs a carpenter to fix it if you haven't forgotten."

Mary turned and looked intently at Lucas.

"Now, tell me all about it. I hear you are writing an account of the life of my son. Is that right?"

THE STORY OF PAUL III

Lucas was about to say something, but Mary continued,

"I am told you are a doctor, am I right? So, before you leave, I hope you will have some advice for me. I have been having dreadful pains in my knees. And, James, you can anoint me with oil and pray for me just like you tell people to do."

James grinned at Lucas.

"As you are a doctor, I expect you want to hear all about my pregnancy. We can start there if you like," said Mary with a twinkle in her eye.

"Well, actually, I'd like to start before this if we can," said Lucas. "I understand from James there was something special about the birth of John the baptiser as well. He was a relative and a little older than Jesus, wasn't he?"

The conversation began, lunch came and went. The shadow of the sun moved across the courtyard and soon the light began to fade. Mary was getting weary, and a little before sunset, James called a halt to the talking. Salome had prepared a supper of fresh baked fish from the lake, and they sat around enjoying the embers of a fire in the courtyard.

There was silence for a while then a slight change in Mary's breathing told them all she had drifted off to sleep. Salome took charge and ushered the men out.

"Come back tomorrow, she has more to tell you." With that, James and Lucas went to their own bedchamber.

"There is so much. I don't know where to begin really," said Lucas as they lay down on their mats to sleep. "She used a beautiful expression earlier. She talked about treasuring all these things in

CHAPTER III

her heart." James started to snore, and Lucas knew it was time to stop talking too.

Lucas rose early the next morning and went out into the courtyard with the sheets of papyrus he had written the day before. He started to put them into order beginning with the announcement to John the baptiser's father Zechariah of the coming of John to Elizabeth in her old age.

Then, there was the visit of the angel Gabriel to Mary in Nazareth and her visit to see Elizabeth. All these bits of personal family information were so precious to Mary. He wrote about the birth itself down in Bethlehem not far from Jerusalem, how she delivered the baby out the back of a crowded inn, how they had huddled together using an animal feeding trough for the new-born baby to sleep in, and then the surprise visitors who turned up in the middle of the night. Lucas was amazed, a group of Judean shepherds of all people. The story was full of little personal touches such as the way they wrapped the baby in the swaddling clothes her mother had sent with her down to Bethlehem.

He was so deeply engrossed in his thoughts, he did not hear Mary enter the courtyard. She stood behind him, then placed her hand gently on his shoulder.

"It's where we keep our most precious things. Our treasury. No one can take it away from us. It goes with me wherever I go, and it is my most valuable possession. Mine is full indeed. My treasury is in my heart, and hardly a day goes by that I do not go there and look at some of those precious, treasured memories."

She struggled to sit down beside Lucas, who helped her settle.

"Oh! My knees. They are so bad these days. Salome is organizing some breakfast and we can eat when James gets up. What do you recommend for my knees, Doctor Lucas?"

"Make a paste of olive oil and some rosemary and mint leaves. Crush them all together and rub it on the hurting joints," suggested Lucas. "If there is any leftover, it goes well with roast lamb."

Mary chuckled at this. "What a practical doctor you are."

"Now, where were we? Oh yes, Jerusalem. Jerusalem is dangerous for most of us these days, so indeed is Galilee," Mary began saying. "Ever since Salome's poor boy, James was killed by the tyrant Herod Agrippa, it has been difficult for us. I don't think she ever got over losing her son. He was such a lovely boy." She paused and wiped her eyes.

"Herod. He was a nasty bit of work, just like the rest of his clan before him. His grandfather was the one who sent his soldiers into Bethlehem looking for us a couple of years after my boy was born. Those poor mothers. It was so terrible, killing all those babies under the age of two. Another of Herod's sons, Herod Antipas, was the one who killed Elizabeth's boy, John. He had my boy sent to him by Pilate."

"I heard about it from my friend Paul, who was a young pharisee and saw the so-called trial," said Lucas.

"Herod Agrippa was another one of the loathsome tribe. He died too, not long after he had poor James beheaded. The foolish man claimed to be God. No wonder he was taken in the way he was."

Mary's eyes filled with tears as she thought of three mothers who had all suffered and lost their sons. After a few moments, Lucas told Mary how John Mark had also recently written an account of the life of Jesus.

CHAPTER III

"He spent a lot of time with Simon Peter, and it was written mostly from Simon's perspective. I have a copy of Mark's scroll, but I left it in Caesarea. They are copying it there, so others can have their own scrolls. I believe it is important we write down as much as we can while people still remember what happened, which is what I am doing too."

"I would like to read it," she said. "I can read, you know. I'm slow, but I can read Greek as long as it isn't too complicated."

Lucas looked slightly embarrassed that he had not brought it with him.

"There is a rip in the last section of the scroll and the end is missing. I hope to find Mark somewhere and get him to add it back. Without the last page, it leaves out the best bit, Jesus rising from the dead."

"We all know he rose and is alive, so it doesn't really matter." Mary answered.

The smell of baking bread wafted through from the house, and shortly breakfast arrived along with Salome. James joined them carrying a bowel of olives and almonds and some hard-boiled eggs.

"How is the writing going?" asked James.

"Very well, we have had some really lovely talks. Haven't we, Mary?" said Lucas through a mouthful of freshly baked bread.

"Yes, indeed we have. But there is one other thing I want to tell you. I think it is important because it was the first time I heard Jesus refer to the Lord God as his father."

Mary ate for a while and when she finished, she started to speak.

"I will never forget the day I heard Jesus call God his Father. It happened when we went as a family to Jerusalem for one of the festivals. I don't remember which one. It was likely fifty years ago now, Jesus would have been about twelve and you had just turned ten," she said looking at James.

"When the feast was over, we headed for home but unbeknown to us, Jesus stayed behind in Jerusalem. We assumed he was with some of the other youngsters in our group. We went a day's journey. We made camp for the night. I had prepared some food and when the children gathered, we realised he was not there. Joseph hadn't seen him all day. I am still surprised he hadn't kept his eye on him. We became concerned, searched for him among our relatives and acquaintances. Somehow, we decided he must have stayed behind in the city. We left all the younger children with the other members of the family and returned to Jerusalem, searching for him."

Mary paused as she remembered the events of so long ago.

"Joseph and I got back to the city late, in the early hours of the morning. It was still dark, and we had no idea where to look. We went to all the people we knew in the city, and no one had seen him. I was beside myself with anxiety. You see, Joseph and I were the only ones who knew who Jesus really was and how special he was. The angel had said he was God's own son and we had been entrusted to care for him and bring him up. Now we had lost him.

"After three days of searching everywhere, I was distraught. We decided to go to the temple. Joseph said we had better go and talk directly with the Lord God and tell him what happened. We went as far as I could go to the Courtyard of the Women in the outer precincts. To our absolute amazement, we found Jesus there, sitting among the teachers, listening to them, and asking them questions. Everyone who was listening to him seemed amazed at his under-

CHAPTER III

standing and his answers. He was right in the middle of them. I wondered where on earth had he been sleeping and what had he been eating.

"We were astonished too. I was so relieved, but we were exhausted emotionally and physically. It was the best part of five days he had been missing. He was only twelve, after all. So, I just blurted out, 'Why have you treated us like this?' I told him his father and I had been in great distress searching for him for days."

Mary's face changed from a look of concern to one of amusement and joy.

"Do you know what he said? I have never forgotten it. He asked us why we had been looking for him. Why had we been searching for him? A twelve-year-old boy, missing for five days. He could have been kidnapped, sold as a slave, murdered, anything. I was so distressed. This was a typical response from a young boy."

Mary chuckled slightly as she told this part of the story.

"Then he said, 'Didn't you know that I must be in my Father's house?'"

She paused, letting the words sink in as Lucas looked at her in his own amazement.

"There was stunned silence. I did not understand initially what he was saying. I think some of those teachers of the Law in the temple did though. They looked shocked and some stared at him because it was blasphemous to describe God as his Father. They looked at him, and then they looked at Joseph and me. We took our son by the hand and Joseph suggested we leave and go home straight away."

"I suppose from their point of view," added James, "here was a twelve-year-old boy not just saying the Lord God was a father but his father. He didn't even call him 'Adonai'."[31]

James reflected on this for a moment or two, then added.

"It is no surprise they were astonished. Years later, Jesus used the same expression when he threw the money changers out of the temple for turning it into a den of robbers. Then, they knew he was calling the Lord God his father for sure because they started to plot to get rid of him around about then, I seem to remember."

Mary nodded and took up the story again.

"So, he came with us, and we went back to Nazareth. He was a good boy and stayed at home with us from then on. He grew into a fine young man. He was such a help to us, and when Joseph died, he was a great support to me and the other children. He never mentioned God being his Father again, but I knew. And he knew. But to everyone else, he was content to be known as the carpenter's son. It was only when he began his public ministry that he started talking about God being his Father. It was one of the many things that got him into so much trouble with the Pharisees and the temple crowd."

There was silence again until Mary finally said,

"As for me, I added these memories to my treasure trove and put them safely away in my heart."

Like Mary, Luke was storing all of these stories in his own treasure trove. He thought of the immense privilege to write them all down. Lucas cleared his throat.

"Umm, is there anyone else you think I should talk to?" asked Lucas.

CHAPTER III

Mary thought for a while, then her eyes lit up as she thought of someone.

"I've just remembered. One of the leaders in this area, Simon, is an old man, older than me," she said smiling. "He was a Pharisee originally. But after he met my son, everything began to change. He often had Jesus at his house for dinners, which caused quite a stir at the time. He lives in a large house on the edge of the town. It has nice views of the lake too…"

Mary was again lost in her thoughts.

CHAPTER IV

A messenger was sent to ask if Simon was able to meet Lucas. An enthusiastic response came back inviting Lucas to come mid-afternoon and to stay for dinner. Simon was indeed an old man, but his memory was still sharp. Lucas instantly took a liking to him and the two quickly withdrew to a shady part of the garden with stunning views over the lake. Simon began to reminisce.

To Lucas' delight and amazement, Simon remembered many of the stories Jesus had told and nearly all were ones he had not heard before. Some, he knew from Mark's account of the life of Jesus, but Simon seemed to know many more.

"How do you remember these stories so well?" asked Lucas.

"It must be the way I was brought up as a Pharisee," answered Simon. "We had to memorise the Law of Moses and much of the rest of the Writings and the Prophets. I know all the Psalms from memory. In Hebrew of course, which won't help you as a Greek too much. Maybe this is why the stories Jesus told stick in my mind. He told quite a few when I was present and some even in my home here as we had meals together."

"I hear he came often," said Lucas. "Are you willing to talk about the times he came to eat at your house?"

CHAPTER IV

Simon looked out across the lake and his face clouded slightly, then he turned to Lucas.

"Yes, I am. Though I was not a gracious host the first time he came."

Simon paused for a while and again gazed out across the lake before turning to Lucas.

"I was rather proud of being a Pharisee back then. It carried a social status with it, and we thought people respected us. Most of us were really proud of our achievements or rather the things we considered were our achievements."

"What were they?" asked Lucas.

"Our main objective was to keep the Torah as best we could. We did not interpret it literally as the Sadducees do, rather we interpreted it in such a way as to make it something we lived by every day to govern our lives. We had a rule for everything. Every eventuality was covered. Nothing was left to personal interpretation.

"When I think about them now and I look at them in the light of what has been revealed to us by Jesus, they truly were more of a burden than we ever realised at the time."

"What do you mean by that?" asked Lucas.

"Let me give you an example," said Simon. "The fourth of God's words to govern our lives says, 'Remember the Sabbath day by keeping it holy. Six days you shall labour and do all your work, but the seventh day is a sabbath to the LORD your God. On it you shall not do any work. For in six days the LORD made the heavens and the earth, the sea, and all that is in them, but he rested on the seventh day. Therefore, the LORD blessed the Sabbath day and made it holy.'

"This is straight forward enough. His intention was for us to rest. I see now he blesses our days of rest. However long ago the Pharisees looked at this and asked the question, 'what is work?' This led them into countless rules and regulations. It resulted in so many restrictions that the Sabbath became a day of great stress and complication rather than rest.

"Some of the rules are ridiculous. Somebody decided wearing a wooden leg on the Sabbath was work. I ask you, how crazy is that? Can you imagine the effort of all those poor people with wooden legs hopping around all day on the Sabbath getting exhausted?"

Simon laughed heartily at the thought as he offered Lucas a top up of wine in his cup.

"This really brought us into conflict with Jesus. He seemed to interpret everything by a new law of love. It was so irritating, and he had a way of seeing through our inconsistencies so quickly. Maybe it was this that drew me to him."

Lucas scratched away with his stylus on sheets of papyrus as Simon opened up.

"I remember one day Jesus was teaching at a friend's house. Some of us were sitting there listening. We had come from every village of Galilee. There were rumours circulating about healings, but I had not witnessed any personally. As Jesus spoke, there was a commotion outside caused by some men who came carrying a paralysed man on a mat. They were trying to take him into the house to lay him before Jesus. When they could not find a way to do this because of the crowd, they went up on the roof, broke a hole in it and lowered him on his mat through the tiles into the middle of the crowd, right

CHAPTER IV

in front of Jesus. You should have heard what my friend said later about the damage to his roof!

"What Jesus said next really shook us. He said to the man on the floor his sins were forgiven. I was stunned by this statement. I thought this was blasphemous as only God can forgive sins. It was as if Jesus knew exactly what we were thinking. He looked straight at me and asked, 'Why are you thinking these things in your hearts? Which is easier to say, 'Your sins are forgiven,' or to say, 'Get up and walk?' I want you to know the Son of Man has authority on earth to forgive sins.' Then he told the paralysed man to get up, take his mat and go home. Immediately, the man stood up in front of us. We were completely amazed and some even gave praise to God. I told a friend we had seen remarkable things that day.[32]

"I had seen a miracle I could not deny. I wanted to meet Jesus myself and talk to him personally. So, I decided to invite him to have dinner with me. He came to my house and was reclining at the table with me and a small group of personally invited friends. The meal was going well. We were chatting and eating, then a woman came into the room. I knew who she was. She worked on the streets. You know what I mean?"

Simon again looked out across the lake. Lucas wondered if Simon was avoiding his eye for some reason. Simon turned and looked directly at Lucas.

"The truth is I more than knew her. I knew her in every sense of the word. I was a young man in those days; my wife had died before we had children. I was lonely and a bit lost. She had come to the house before, and she knew her way into the dining area. I think I may have even told her Jesus was coming. She walked in carrying an alabaster jar of perfume. I was embarrassed for this to happen at my table. I was about to call my steward to have her removed when she went and stood behind Jesus and began weeping copiously. Her tears wet his feet, and then she wiped them with her hair. She kissed them and poured perfume on them. It was shocking. I had not treated Jesus well. I had not provided water for his feet when he arrived, and here was this woman…" Again, Simon looked out across the lake.

"I began thinking to myself *if this man were a prophet as people were saying, he would know what kind of woman she was.* I felt so angry with her and indignant she had done this in my house in front of my friends. I was thinking Jesus should have pushed her away, but he did not. He just let her do it. I can tell you; you could have cut through the atmosphere in the room.

"I'll never forget what Jesus said to me. He looked straight at me in his unique way and said, 'Simon, I have something to tell you.' I immediately thought this would discharge the situation, so I asked him to tell me so at least we could ignore this woman.

"Jesus then started talking about two people who owed money to a moneylender. One owed him five hundred denarii and the other fifty. Neither of them had the money to pay the moneylender back, so he forgave the debts of both. Then came the question, which of them would love him more?

"I replied, I supposed the one who had the bigger debt forgiven. 'You have judged correctly,' Jesus said to me. Then he turned toward the woman and said to me, 'Do you see this woman, Simon? I came into your house. You did not give me any water for my feet, but she wet my feet with her tears and wiped them with her hair. You did not give me a kiss, but this woman, from the time she entered, has not stopped kissing my feet. You did not put oil on my head, but she

CHAPTER IV

has poured perfume on my feet. Her many sins have been forgiven as her great love has shown. But whoever has been forgiven little loves little.' Then Jesus said to her, 'Your sins are forgiven'.

"This caused a great stir among my guests who were asking each other, 'Who is this who even forgives sins?' I had heard him say this the first time I saw him heal the paralysed man. Now here he was saying it again to this woman, right in my home. Then to my amazement, Jesus said to the woman, 'Your faith has saved you. Go in peace.'[33]

"I was deeply troubled by this. Jesus was unlike any other rabbi or teacher I had ever heard. I could not get these thoughts out of my mind. I was drawn to him and wanted to hear more."

Simon continued talking as Lucas made more notes.

"One Sabbath, Jesus went to eat in the house of one of the most prominent Pharisees in Galilee. I was also invited to be a guest. One of the guests was not well, suffering from abnormal swelling of his body. His legs were terribly swollen. Jesus asked us Pharisees who considered ourselves experts in the Law. 'Is it lawful to heal on the Sabbath or not?' he asked, but we all remained silent. Taking hold of the man, he healed him and sent him home.

"Then Jesus asked us if any of us had an ox or a child who falls into a well on the Sabbath day, would we not immediately pull it out? Of course, we would. We had nothing to say. It was going to be another one of those difficult meals. I wonder sometimes why we Pharisees kept inviting him to dinner. We were beginning to hear he would also eat with undesirable types, you know, tax collectors and the like. My heart was in such turmoil in those days. I was hearing things that challenged me to the core of my being. Jesus spoke like no one else I had ever heard and with such authority.

"I digress. Where was I?" asked Simon.

"You were talking about the time Jesus dined with a group of you on the Sabbath day. Can I ask? Wasn't this against your rules about Sabbath breaking?" asked Lucas.

Simon laughed quietly.

"Exactly," he said. "This is the whole problem of pharisaical behaviour. We had rules for everything, and we found ways to get around our own rules when it suited us. In this case, it was a cold meal prepared the day before, so no one had to work on the Sabbath.

"Let me continue. When Jesus noticed how the guests picked places of honour at the table, he told them one of his stories. He said, 'When someone invites you to a wedding feast, do not take the place of honour, for a person more distinguished than you may have been invited. If so, the host who invited both of you will come and say to you, 'Give this person your seat.' Then, humiliated, you will have to take the least important place. So, when you are invited, take the lowest place, so that when your host comes, he will say to you, 'Friend, move up to a better place.' Then you will be honoured in the presence of all the other guests. For all those who exalt themselves will be humbled, and those who humble themselves will be exalted.'

"Then Jesus turned to the host and said, 'When you give a luncheon or dinner, do not invite your friends, your brothers or sisters, your relatives, or your rich neighbours. If you do, they may invite you back and so you will be repaid. Rather, when you give a banquet, invite the poor, the crippled, the lame, the blind, and you will be blessed. Although they cannot repay you, you will be repaid at the resurrection of the righteous.'

CHAPTER IV

"When one of those sitting close to him at the table heard this, he said to Jesus, 'Blessed is the one who will eat at the feast in the kingdom of God.' He sounded so sanctimonious; it made me almost choke on my food.

"Jesus replied by telling yet another story: 'A certain man was preparing a great banquet and invited many guests. At the time of the banquet, he sent his servant to tell those who had been invited, 'Come, for everything is now ready.' However, they all began to make excuses. The first said, 'I have just bought a field, and I must go and see it. Please excuse me.' Another said, 'I have just bought five yokes of oxen, and I'm on my way to try them out. Please excuse me.' Still another said, 'I just got married, so I can't come.' The servant came back and reported this to his master.

"This is how these stories unfold," added Simon. "We could identify ourselves in the stories. We all make excuses like this if we don't think the invite is from someone important enough. Jesus continued, 'Then the owner of the house became angry and ordered his servant, 'Go out quickly into the streets and alleys of the town and bring in the poor, the crippled, the blind and the lame.'

"'Sir,' the servant said, 'what you ordered has been done, but there is still room.' Then the master told his servant, 'Go out to the roads and country lanes and compel them to come in, so that my house will be full. I tell you, not one of those who were invited will get a taste of my banquet.'[34]

"We knew exactly what he was getting at. It was a memorable meal, I tell you." Simon stood and stretched. "Now all this talk of meals and banquets has made me hungry. I am sure you must be as well, Lucas. Come, let us go back inside and eat together. There is another story I want to tell you about. It could take a while, so let's refresh ourselves."

Lucas and Simon walked slowly back to the house as Simon continued to tell anecdotes and stories about Jesus. In the dining area of Simon's spacious home, a meal was spread. Lucas looked around the room and turned to Simon.

"Is this...?"

Before Lucas could finish his question, Simon interrupted.

"Yes, this is exactly the room where it happened. She came through the door there. And I want you to recline here next to me. It is just where Jesus reclined.

"I'm not sure when it was, but sometime later the same year, we started to hear rumours of Jesus going to visit the homes of tax collectors and other undesirables. I remember thinking at the time, our contact with Jesus was getting difficult as we felt contaminated by his seemingly total disregard for our religious standards.

"The occasion I want to tell you about happened in the main market square in the town in front of everyone."

"Which town are you talking about?" asked Lucas.

"Here, in Capernaum," answered Simon. "On this occasion, there was quite a crowd which included many tax collectors and a group of people we just called 'sinners.' These were just about everyone we Pharisees disapproved of. Everyone was gathering around to hear what Jesus had to say. There was also quite a large group of us Pharisees and teachers of the law. We were standing on the edge of the crowd so as not to be contaminated by getting too close to the riff raff.

"There was a lot of muttering going on about Jesus welcoming

CHAPTER IV

sinners and eating meals with them. I was there with them, but by now I am not sure whether they considered me one of the sinners because I had eaten with Jesus a few times. Again, it was as if he knew exactly what we were all thinking. He talked generally and laughed at some of the comments people were calling out.

"You know something, Lucas. He was one of the most relaxed people I ever met. He just seemed to be at peace, and it showed whenever he spoke. He smiled and laughed a lot too. One of his disciples once told me when Jesus prayed, he almost jumped for joy; he was so happy. As if he was sharing a glorious joke with his heavenly Father.

"But I digress. On this occasion, he told three stories. The first was about a lost sheep."

"Is this the story about a shepherd who lost one of his sheep out of a flock of one hundred and went looking for it?" asked Lucas.

"Yes, that's the story," answered Simon.

"I have heard this one too," said Lucas. "Mark has it in his account of Jesus' life. But forgive me, please continue."

"The second story was about a woman who had lost a precious and valuable coin off her dowry chain. She looked everywhere for it and only when she lit a lamp, did she find it in a corner of her house. Jesus said she was so happy she called all her friends and neighbours to tell them she had found it. I'll never forget what he said next, 'In the same way, I tell you, there is rejoicing in the presence of the angels of God over one sinner who repents.' This was not lost on me. I had already judged the sinners around us and here was Jesus saying heaven rejoiced about them being found. After he said this, he looked straight at me.

"The third story he told us changed my life forever. It was about a man who had two sons."[35]

Lucas listened as Simon recounted the story. He knew every word as if he had told it many times before. Lucas did not write a word down. He listened, captivated by the words and the way in which Simon spoke. After he finished the story, the two men sat in silence letting the impact of the words settle in their hearts. Simon broke the silence again by adding,

"It is the best story I have ever heard. I would say from that day, I was truly his follower."

"Would you write it down for me? Just as you told it to me. I would not want to take anything away from it," asked Lucas.

"Of course, I will, with pleasure."

Simon became reflective as the memory played in his mind.

"As Jesus spoke, I felt at times I was like the younger son who was coming home to his father. In the second half of the story, I saw myself as the self-righteous older brother. As he spoke, I knew he was describing the way God was like a father to us. It was so clear. When he finished telling the story, in my heart I stopped being a Pharisee. I lost all interest in my former life of dead religious legalism. I withdrew from many of my former friends because they were moving in the opposite direction. They started to actively attack and seek to silence Jesus.

"Much later, after Jesus was arrested and executed, I started to hear rumours he had come back to life. I made my way up to Jerusalem and contacted his friends and family there. One day there was a huge crowd of us, at least five hundred people, and he came and spoke with us. He really was alive. Not long after, I was with them

CHAPTER IV

again in the city at the time of Pentecost. You know what happened on that day. It blew the last shred of my pharisaical mind to bits! I became a Follower of the Way."

∿∿∿

James returned to Jerusalem while Lucas stayed in Capernaum for several weeks. He spent a lot of time in further conversation with Simon the former Pharisee and gathered more stories about the time Jesus spent in Galilee. Simon may have abandoned his pharisaical lifestyle but his mind was sharp and his memory as keen as ever.

Together, they wrote down a considerable amount of material about things Jesus taught and said.

Simon, the former Pharisee, was a priceless resource.

CHAPTER V

After another brief visit to Lysias in Tiberius, Lucas returned to Caesarea five months after he left. The journey was short but winter had come and the roads were difficult. Lysias had provided Lucas with a pack horse to transport his increasing collection of papyrus manuscripts and canvasses to keep them dry. As soon as he entered the city, he went straight to Theophilus' house. They greeted one another and Lucas asked after Paul.

"He is in good health. In fact, he is better than he has been for a long time," said Theophilus.

"Any news of his trial yet?" asked Lucas.

"Nothing, although Felix and his wife are here. They came about a month ago. Apparently, they prefer the weather down here in the winter. He sent for Paul, and they had quite a long talk. But nothing came out of it. Felix is still more interested in trying to get a bribe from Paul to get out of custody. There is no news from Jerusalem in terms of any charges. It seems everyone has gone to bed for the winter," said Theophilus. Then he added. "I think Paul is bored though; it's been almost eight months since his arrest. I am sure he will be delighted to see you."

Later the same day, Lucas went to visit Paul and found him wrapped in a blanket in front of a brazier. In his hands were a copy

CHAPTER V

of one of the Jewish writings, and he was straining in the poor light to read the words. He turned and looked towards the door as Lucas entered.

"Who is there? I can't see well in this light," Paul said.

"It's me," said Lucas.

"Lucas! My dear boy! Oh! I am so glad to see you. When did you get back?"

"I arrived earlier today. I came through the Jezreel valley from Galilee and down the coast road. It is so good to be back. And how are you, my friend? It looks to me you are struggling with your eyesight. It's no surprise, trying to read in this light."

"Nothing changes much as far as my eyes are concerned. Normally, I get Tychicus to read to me, but sadly, he doesn't read Hebrew. When I am dictating and I quote the Hebrew scriptures, I usually translate them into Greek as I go. Sometimes I quote from the Greek translation of the Scriptures so he can write them in my letters, but enough about me." Paul became more animated as he talked. "How are you? I want to know all about your travels and who you met in Galilee."

The two friends sat for hours as Lucas recounted his time in Galilee. When the sun set, Lucas departed having promised Paul he would come back with his manuscripts and read to him the stories he had written down.

The next morning, Lucas returned with a large bundle of papyrus manuscripts. He had organised them overnight and beginning with the stories from Mary, he read them to Paul.

"These are such precious memories," said Paul when Lucas put the last manuscript down. "As you read them to me, I could feel the presence of the Spirit in the words, Lucas. It was as if the Holy Spirit himself was breathing through them. I think the Spirit has been leading you to meet people and to hear their stories. I am not exaggerating, but what you are writing will be a priceless gift to all who read them."

Lucas blushed, embarrassed by Paul's words.

"I am just writing what I hear Paul," he said.

"Exactly! And you are hearing the prompting of the Spirit as you listen and as you write. You must complete this great work God has given you. I will ask Tychicus to assist you as much as you need him. I am sure there will be room for you both in your scriptorium at Theophilus' house.

"What you are doing is not just writing an account of the life of Jesus. No, you are pointing to who Jesus is through these encounters and stories. This is what the Holy Spirit is inspiring you to do. He breathes truth and life into you and the things you are hearing. You then breathe out these inspired truths through your words and thoughts he has put in you, and this testifies to who Jesus is. It is a partnership with the Father and the Spirit to point your readers to who Jesus of Nazareth is, the Messiah, the son of God."

Lucas sat in silence staring at Paul as the weight of these words sunk into his heart. Some time ago he realised that beyond telling a story, what he was discovering would point people to the truth about who Jesus really was. The stories had become a means of explaining truth.

"Can I ask you a question about something you said yesterday?" asked Lucas.

CHAPTER V

Paul nodded.

"When I was talking to people like James, Jesus' brother, and Simon, the former Pharisee, they sometimes quoted the Hebrew Scriptures in Greek. It seems they freely translated as they go along. You said you did this too. Simon had a copy of the Torah in Greek."

"Yes, it would be the Translation of the Seventy," said Paul. "I know it well. It was produced by Jewish rabbis and scholars in Alexandria over two hundred years ago. As you know, it's widely used by Greek speaking Jews all over the empire. I occasionally use it when I quote the Hebrew Scriptures in my letters. However, sometimes the rabbis interpreted according to their opinions rather than an accurate translation. To be honest, it's a good version but sometimes I change it to a better translation when I use it in my letters."

"You change it?" Lucas looked surprised. "But if it is the words of God, isn't it wrong to change it?"

"Who said it is God's words?" asked Paul.

"But I thought this is what you teach?"

"Not all the words in the Hebrew writings are God's words. There are also words of people, like Job's friends, who the Lord God disagrees with. There are the words of the evil one in the garden of Eden and in Job. There are even the words of God's enemies. Yet the incidents and how people understood them at the time become God's word to us. They point to Jesus and reveal him. As the eyes of our hearts are enlightened, we receive revelation from the Father."

"I met a man in Jerusalem who told me an interesting story about an encounter he had with Jesus after he was raised from the dead. He talked like this too," said Lucas.

"Oh? Who was this man?" asked Paul.

"His name is Cleopas; he lives in Emmaus. He is quite old now but clearly remembers the encounter he had. He told me on the day Jesus rose from the dead, he and a friend were going home to his village about seven miles from Jerusalem. He said they were talking about everything that had happened. As they discussed these things, he said Jesus himself came up and walked along with them. But they didn't recognize him."

"What do you mean they didn't recognise him?" asked Paul.

"He said it seemed as if somehow they were initially kept from recognising him. Anyway, Jesus asked them, 'What are you discussing as you walk along?'

"Cleopas said they stopped and looked sadly at each other, then said to Jesus, 'Are you the only one visiting Jerusalem who does not know the things that have happened here in these days?' Then Jesus asked, 'What things?' Cleopas told me how he explained all that had gone on and how their hopes of Jesus being the Messiah had been dashed when he was crucified. Then he talked about what happened on the third day, about the women seeing angels and the empty tomb."

"This was on the evening of the same day?" asked Paul.

"Yes," answered Lucas, "the same evening. Then Jesus said to them, 'How foolish you are, and how slow to believe all the prophets have spoken. Didn't the Messiah have to suffer these things and then enter his glory?' And beginning with Moses and all the Prophets, he carefully explained to them what was said in all the Scriptures concerning himself."

Lucas stopped after he recounted this part of the story.

CHAPTER V

Then he said,

"This is what you are saying too, Paul. The Hebrew Scriptures point to Jesus."

Lucas continued telling Cleopas' story of how when they reached their home, they invited Jesus in to eat with them as it was evening.

"Cleopas said when they sat at the table to eat, Jesus took bread, gave thanks, and broke it. Then, he offered it to them. It was only then their eyes were opened, and they recognized him. Then he disappeared from their sight.

"It was what was said next that really struck me," said Lucas. "They asked each other, 'Were not our hearts burning within us while he talked with us on the road and opened the Scriptures to us?' I am beginning to see more clearly how the Scriptures point to Jesus and reveal him and things not seen before are made clear. When it impacts our hearts, we really see the truth."[36]

"This is how revelation works, Lucas. We see with the eyes of our hearts what we cannot see with our minds. The Father gives this gift to us. God's Spirit indeed breathes the life of God through these writings and Scriptures," said Paul. "They become useful for teaching us, giving evidence, and correcting us and training us in righteousness, so that God's servants may be thoroughly equipped for every good work. It is how I understand the sacred writings we, Jews, have been entrusted with."

"What do you mean by 'giving evidence'? asked Lucas.

"They provide evidence of who Jesus is. In the same way Jesus himself explained things to Cleopas in your story," said Paul.

"Do you think, Paul, the letters you have written, the letter written to the Hebrews, James' letter and even the account of the Jesus' life by Mark are similar to the sacred writings of the Jews? God's Spirit breathing through them too?" asked Lucas.

Paul sat for a few minutes saying nothing, staring into the distance. Finally, he turned and looked at Lucas.

"I think you need to get on with writing your version of the events of Jesus' life. It sounds to me it will be good news for those who read it and maybe as the Spirit leads, it will be more than that. Now go back to Theophilus' house and get to work, my good doctor. What does he call you? Luke?"

∿∿∿

Over the next few weeks, Lucas spent many hours at Theophilus' house in his writing room organising his manuscripts and painstakingly putting them together. He used Mark's work as the backbone for his version adding sections and details he had gleaned through his own investigations. Everyone in the community of believers in Caesarea were aware of Lucas' task and encouraged and supported him. Tychicus spent time helping and copying completed sections.

One day, Zacchaeus arrived having been away in Jerusalem. He was accompanied by an elderly man who Lucas instantly recognised.

"Cleopas! How wonderful to see you, and Zacchaeus too. Welcome back! I am so pleased you are here."

"I have been hearing from Zacchaeus about your great work and I wanted to come and see you and encourage you," said Cleopas.

"This is perfect timing," said Lucas. "I have almost come to the end of my work, and I have been writing down the story you told

CHAPTER V

me about your meeting with Jesus on the way to your home in Emmaus. I would like you to check the details for me."

"With pleasure," replied Cleopas.

"Come sit here beside me," said Lucas. "Tychicus, please clear those manuscripts from the chair so Cleopas can sit."

The old man settled into the chair and was soon avidly reading aloud from the manuscript. Then he turned to Lucas.

"May I tell you what happened when we went back to Jerusalem to tell the Eleven we had met Jesus?" asked Cleopas.

"Yes, please do. I am eager to hear it," said Lucas.

Everyone in the room went silent as they sat and began to listen to Cleopas. Lucas took up a stylus to write notes.

"We returned at once to Jerusalem. We found the Eleven and those with them assembled. They told us, 'It is true! The Lord has risen and has appeared to Simon,'" said Cleopas.

"Then we told them what happened on the way, and how we recognized Jesus when he broke the bread. While we were talking about this, Jesus himself stood among us and said to us, 'Peace be with you.' Everyone was startled and some were frightened, thinking they were seeing a ghost.

"Jesus said to us, 'Why are you troubled, and why does doubt rise in your minds? Look at my hands and my feet. It is I, touch me and see. A ghost does not have flesh and bones as you see I have.'

"When he said this, he showed us his hands and feet. Some still did not believe, others were overjoyed and amazed. He asked us, 'Do you have anything here to eat?' Someone gave him a piece of grilled fish, and he took it and ate it in our presence.

"When he finished eating, he said to us, 'This is what I told you while I was still with you: Everything must be fulfilled that is written about me in the Law of Moses, the Prophets and the Psalms.'

"As he spoke to us, our minds started to open, and we began to understand the Scriptures. He told us, 'This is what is written: The Messiah will suffer and rise from the dead on the third day, and repentance for the forgiveness of sins will be preached in his name to all nations, beginning at Jerusalem. You are witnesses of these things. I am going to send you what my Father has promised, but stay in the city until you have been clothed with power from on high.'"[37]

As Cleopas stopped speaking, there was a deep sense of the presence of the Spirit in the room. Other than the gentle scratching of Lucas' stylus on the papyrus, no one dared speak.

CHAPTER VI

As winter turned into spring, and the unpredictable storms of the winter season ended, the port in Caesarea slowly filled with merchant ships and the occasional naval galley. Caesarea Maritima was a major hub for trade from the east and the centre of Roman administration in the Province of Judea. With the arrival of ships and galleys came not only goods and merchandise but also passengers and mail from Rome and other places across the empire. The wharfs and docks of the port were crowded with all manner of cargo being unloaded and loaded.

A large merchant ship slowly edged past the northern of the two huge artificial breakwaters forming the harbour built by King Herod over fifty years before. The ship typically came down from the north hugging the coast. As soon as it had berthed, slaves from the docks swarmed across the gunwales to unload its cargo. Passengers pushed through the crowded decks and jumped ashore. An older man was helped ashore by a younger man who accompanied him. Two others with them carried their baggage.

The group made their way from the harbour area through the warehouses and walked purposefully along the main thoroughfare of the city, branching off to the south away from the busy commercial district and the forum into a residential area. They stopped

THE STORY OF PAUL III

outside Philip's house and knocked on the heavy wooden door. A few moments later, the door opened from within and a woman exclaimed loudly with joy.

"Simon Peter! How wonderful! Come in! Come in, I will go and call my father. It is so good to see you again."

Peter and his companions slipped in through the gate and went along the corridor leading into the inner courtyard. It was a loud and joyful reunion as Philip appeared with another of his daughters.

"Peter, my dear, dear friend! How good to see you. It has been so long," said Philip. "And John Mark! You too. I am delighted to have you in my home. Come in, all of you. Girls, quickly let us get food and something to refresh our guests."

There was so much to talk about; so much news to share and hear as they sat down to eat and drink together.

"News about Paul has reached us," said Peter. "We come with gifts to help support him. Is he still here? Is he well?"

The questions tumbled out and Philip reported on Paul's condition in Herod's palace across the city. Peter and Mark were relieved Paul was well, even if he was still in captivity.

"It's been a year now," said Philip. "He is still waiting for some decision from the governor who seems to show no willingness to release him. Felix knows Paul has many friends here and we know he is hoping to extract money from us to release him, but Paul has forbidden us to pay anything."

"I want to see him as soon as possible, both of us, me and Mark. Can it be arranged?" asked Peter.

"I will send a messenger to Paul, and we can arrange it for

CHAPTER VI

tomorrow," said Philip. "Did you know Paul's travelling companion Lucas is here also? He stayed when the other brothers returned home last year."

At this news, Mark became excited.

"This is wonderful news," said Mark. "I met him some years ago when we were in Ephesus, and we talked about his interest in writing an account of the life of Jesus. Do you know if he has done it?"

"Oh, yes. He has been busy over these last few months. I know he will be delighted to see you. He is staying at Theophilus' house, and they are using it as a place to write and make copies of the manuscripts of Paul's letters. We must contact him so you can see what he has done."

The next few days were a time of many reunions. Paul was overjoyed to see Peter and John Mark. Lucas was particularly happy to see Mark. News was shared of friends in Ephesus and Macedonia. Paul was greatly encouraged by Peter's visit. Cornelius was also delighted to meet Peter again.

Lucas sat with Mark one afternoon and talked about his visits to Galilee and the people he had met. Mark listened with great interest. Lucas stopped talking and then finally addressed an important issue for him.

"Marcus, my friend, I have a request."

"What is it?" asked Mark. "How can I help?"

Lucas looked slightly awkward, then he said,

"I would like to build my account of the ministry of Jesus around your version. I have a collection of stories, but I am not sure when they happened and in what order. However, your account gives me a pattern to follow and where to fit them in. I can't think of a better way of doing it. I don't want to steal your work. I just think you have given us such a wonderful account and I want to add the eyewitness accounts I have together with it. Does this make sense? How would you feel about me doing this?"

"My dear friend, I would be delighted. The more we can spread this good news, the better. In fact, I heard from Apollos, who is in Alexandria these days, that Matthaeus, the tax collector who was one of Jesus' closest followers, is also writing an account. Like you, I believe this is important."

∿∿∿

Peter wanted to revisit several people and groups of followers of Jesus in the area, so he and Mark stayed in Caesarea for almost two weeks. His plan from there was to travel to Jerusalem and visit family and friends in Galilee.

Lucas spent time with Mark putting the finishing touches to his great work about Jesus. When he finished, Lucas invited his host Theophilus to the scriptorium.

"I have completed my work," he said. "But there is one last thing I want to do."

"How can I help you?" asked Theophilus.

"You have helped me more than you will ever know, my dear friend. However, I want to read you the opening lines. Please sit down and let me read them to you."

Theophilus sat on a stool across the desk from Lucas, who unrolled the large manuscript. Lucas found the opening lines and read aloud.

CHAPTER VI

"Many have undertaken to draw up an account of the things that have been fulfilled among us, just as they were handed down to us by those who from the first were eyewitnesses and servants of the word. With this in mind, since I myself have carefully investigated everything from the beginning, I too decided to write an orderly account for you, most excellent Theophilus, so that you may know the certainty of the things you have been taught."[38]

Tears welled in Theophilus' eyes and rolled down his cheeks.

"I am not worthy of this dedication, Luke," said Theophilus.

"It has nothing to do with being worthy, Theo. I have dedicated it to you out of love and appreciation for you, my dear friend, and, because like me, you are a Gentile by birth and we, Gentiles, need to read these things so we can know with certainty the truth we have been taught."

Lucas stood and went over to where Theophilus sat with his head in his hands. He knelt beside his friend and put his arms around him. Theophilus sobbed deeply.

∿∿∿

Before Peter departed for Jerusalem, Lucas invited him to his lodgings at Theophilus' house. He explained to Peter about his two projects. He had finished the major work about Jesus, but it was the other project he wanted to discuss with Peter.

"I am also writing about what happened after Jesus rose from the dead and returned to his Father in heaven. I know Jesus told you all to wait in Jerusalem until the Holy Spirit was sent by the Father. Am I right in saying he said, 'You will receive power when the Holy Spirit comes on you; and you will be my witnesses in Jerusalem,

THE STORY OF PAUL III

and in all Judea and Samaria, and to the ends of the earth.' Is this what he said?"

"Yes, they are the exact words he spoke. How do you know this?" asked Peter.

"I have heard them from James and also Zacchaeus. I have bits and pieces of the story from some people, but everyone says I need to talk to you. Would you be willing to tell me about those early days?"

Peter listened intently to what Lucas had to say. He closed his eyes for a while as if he was praying. Then he opened them and looked directly at Lucas.

"I knew Father had a reason for me to come to Judea at this time, but I was not sure what it was. I said to John Mark, I sensed the Spirit was prompting me to come here. I did not know you were here. Now I know why I needed to come. I am delighted to help you in whatever way I can. Maybe we could go to Jerusalem together so you can see the places where many of these things occurred."

"Thank you, Peter. This will be wonderful. I know the story has only just begun in many ways. I know about Paul's journeys and Philip's meeting with the Ethiopian official, also Cornelius' conversion, but there are many things I have heard about you. I would love to hear these things directly from you."

This conversation was the start of a new journey of discovery for Lucas. He shared with Paul his plan and received enthusiastic encouragement from him. He also talked with Tychicus who willingly agreed to make a copy of his manuscript. Within a few days, Lucas set off with Simon Peter and John Mark for Jerusalem.

CHAPTER VII

Soon after Lucas and Peter departed for Jerusalem, another ship docked in the port with passengers aboard. It had come from Macedonia and stopped at Ephesus on route where it took on more passengers. Upon arriving at Caesarea, two of the passengers who disembarked quickly made their way into the city and went straight to Philip's house. They were two of Paul's close friends, Aristarchus and Titus. Both men brought news of the communities of believers around the Aegean Sea: Corinth, Macedonia, Ephesus, and the communities inland at Colossae and Laodicea.

They met Paul in his prison cell in Herod's palace, and there was great rejoicing. There was news from Timothy, and Aquila and Priscilla and many others. Paul was encouraged.

"It makes my heart so glad to hear this news," said Paul. "I long to see them all. Maybe one day I will be able to go back. But only God knows when that might be. In many ways, I am frustrated by being held here. None of the authorities seem to want to settle my case." He sighed.

"Have you thought of writing to our brothers back in Macedonia and Ephesus to encourage them?" asked Aristarchus. "Not to sort out problems but to bless them."

"It is something I have been thinking about these many months," said Paul. "I have had time to think about what I teach and what Father has shown me. I remember when he spoke to me on the road outside Damascus. I recall he told me to be a witness of what I had seen and what he would show me. Throughout the years, since then, I feel so privileged because he has poured revelation into my heart."

This conversation stirred something in Paul's heart, giving form to something he had been thinking about. He felt the familiar whisper and anointing of the Spirit welling up within him. He woke one night with the strong sense of God's presence in his room, speaking to his heart. He began to contemplate the enormous gift God the Father had poured out upon his sons and daughters. Paul began to see how God, who was eternally Father, had planned even before the creation of the world to have sons whom he could pour his love upon.

When he woke the next morning, his fingers were itching to find a pen. He knew he needed help. He asked the guard to send a message to his friends. Paul paced up and down in his cell as revelation filled his heart. An hour or so later, Tychicus, Titus and Aristarchus arrived out of breath carrying a bag full of new papyrus manuscripts, styluses, and ink.

"We got your message. We brought the things you requested. What is so urgent?" Titus asked.

"I have to write to our friends, to the people you have been telling me about. I have been up for hours. I know I must do this now," said Paul.

Tychicus had never seen Paul like this. He recognised the urgency in his words and in his body language. But this was something new. He quickly made some space on the table in the room putting

CHAPTER VII

Paul's half eaten breakfast on the floor. He sharpened the point of the stylus and dipped it in fresh ink.

"Okay, Paul, I'm ready when you are," said Tychicus.

"Paul, an apostle of Christ Jesus by the will of God, to God's holy people, the faithful in Christ Jesus. Grace and peace to you from God our Father and the Lord Jesus Christ," began Paul.[39]

"Who is this being sent to?" asked Tychicus, "The community in Ephesus?"

"I am not sure at this point," said Paul. "Maybe it is to a wider group. I am sure the Spirit will make it clear to us."

As Paul spoke, the power of God flowed through his heart, into his mind and the words tumbled out of his mouth one after the other. He barely paused for a breath. Tychicus struggled to keep up as his stylus shot across the sheet of papyrus. At one point, he asked Paul to slow down but it was as if Paul could not hear him. The words came thick and fast, without obvious punctuation. It was an astonishing flow of revelation.

"Praise be to the God and Father of our Lord Jesus Christ, who has blessed us in the heavenly realms with every spiritual blessing in Christ, for he chose us in him before the creation of the world to be holy and blameless in his sight, in love he planned for us to be placed as his sons through Jesus Christ, in accordance with his pleasure and will, to the praise of his glorious grace, which he has freely given us in the One he loves...."

Paul was pacing up and down the room, his breathing heavy as the words kept coming.

"... in him we have redemption through his blood, the forgiveness of sins, in accordance with the riches of God's grace that he lavished on us with all wisdom and understanding, he made known to us the mystery of his will according to his good pleasure, which he purposed in Christ, to be put into effect when the times reach their fulfilment to bring unity to all things in heaven and on earth under Christ, in him we were also chosen, having been predestined according to the plan of him who works out everything in conformity with the purpose of his will, in order that we, who were the first to put our hope in Christ, might be for the praise of his glory and you also were included in Christ when you heard the message of truth, the gospel of your salvation when you believed, you were marked in him with a seal, the promised Holy Spirit, who is a deposit guaranteeing our inheritance until the redemption of those who are God's possession to the praise of his glory."[40]

Finally, Paul stopped. He staggered and started to collapse on the floor under the anointing of the Holy Spirit. Aristarchus quickly stepped forward and caught him, gently lowering him to the ground. Paul's eyes were closed, and he was sweating.

"Are you alright, Paul?" asked Aristarchus. "Do you feel unwell?"

"No, I'm fine. I was overwhelmed. I couldn't stop. Tychicus, we will need to look at it together later in case you missed something," said Paul. "I'm really alright. Let's continue."

Paul changed direction. He started to pray for all those who would receive the letter. He had heard about their faith and some of them he knew personally. He prayed that the God of the Lord Jesus, who he called 'the glorious Father' would give them the Spirit of wisdom and revelation to know the Father better. He prayed that the eyes of their hearts would be enlightened. As he spoke, the flow of revelation continued, and he poured out the truth God had revealed to him.[41]

CHAPTER VII

Over the next few days Paul continued to dictate to Tychicus. Pictures and images added understanding to the revelation he was receiving. He remembered the inscription on the wall in the temple in Jerusalem forbidding Gentiles from entering further into the temple, dividing them from the people of Israel. So, he wrote,

"But now in Christ Jesus, you who once were far away have been brought near by the blood of Christ. For he himself is our peace, who has made the two groups one and has destroyed the barrier, the dividing wall of hostility, by setting aside in his flesh the law with its commands and regulations. His purpose was to create in himself one new humanity out of the two, thus making peace, and in one body to reconcile both of them to God through the cross, by which he put to death their hostility. He came and preached peace to you who were far away and peace to those who were near. For through him we both have access to the Father by one Spirit."[42]

"I have never seen it like this, Paul," said Tychicus. "I always thought we, Gentiles, would always be separated from you Jews. Two groups within the community of believers but so different. Yet here you are saying Jesus has come to create a new race, a new humanity. We become one, reconciled by the death of Jesus on the cross. This is astonishing."

"Consequently," said Paul, "you are no longer foreigners and strangers, but fellow citizens with God's people and also members of his household, built on the foundation of the apostles and prophets, with Christ Jesus himself as the chief cornerstone. In him, the whole building is joined together and rises to become a holy temple in the Lord. And in him, you too are being built together to become a dwelling in which God lives by his Spirit."[43]

"I need a break, Paul," said Tychicus choking back tears.

He put down the stylus and covered his face with his hands, quietly weeping.

"I have felt a foreigner all my life," said Tychicus. "I was taken as a young boy from my family. I became a slave. I learned to read and write and eventually when my master died, I was freed as a gesture of appreciation for how I had served. But I never felt I belonged. I always felt a stranger and a foreigner. Even when I was found by Jesus and I became one of his followers, I never really felt I truly belonged. Even more so when those Pharisees started saying we Gentiles were not real believers and we needed to be circumcised. More separation and alienation. What you are saying here is life changing. This is truly the message of a Father who is uniting us into one new man in Christ. It is like a great mystery that had been hidden and is now revealed. Thank you, Paul, thank you."

"I am not quite finished yet," said Paul. I have more I feel the Spirit wants to say on this. Are you ready, my son?"

"For this reason, I, Paul, the prisoner of Christ Jesus for the sake of you, Gentiles."

Paul stopped as another thought came to him.

"Surely you have heard about the administration of God's grace that was given to me for you, that is, the mystery made known to me by revelation, as I have already written briefly. In reading this, then, you will be able to understand my insight into the mystery of Christ, which was not made known to people in other generations as it has now been revealed by the Spirit to God's holy apostles and prophets. This mystery is that through the gospel, the Gentiles are heirs together with Israel, members together of one body, and sharers together in the promise in Christ Jesus."[44]

CHAPTER VII

The three Gentile believers in the room looked at one another in amazement as Paul dictated. Tychicus wrote down each word. Titus stood and looked out the window of the cell. He could see slaves and soldiers in the palace courtyard going about their business oblivious to the importance of what was happening in the cell not far from them.

"They don't know it yet, but each one of them out there can become heirs and members of the one body and have a share in the promise in Jesus," said Titus. "We have a lot of work to do still."

"I became a servant of this gospel by the gift of God's grace given me through the working of his power," said Paul. "Although I am less than the least of all the Lord's people, this grace was given me: to preach to the Gentiles the boundless riches of Christ, and to make plain to everyone the administration of this mystery, which for ages past was kept hidden in God, who created all things."

Paul paused as if he were lost in thought. Then he continued.

"His intent was that now, through the assemblies of believers, the manifold wisdom of God should be made known to the rulers and authorities in the heavenly realms, according to his eternal purpose that he accomplished in Christ Jesus our Lord. In him and through faith in him, we may approach God with freedom and confidence. I ask you, therefore, not to be discouraged because of my sufferings for you, which are your glory."[45]

"What we are about is not just impacting people in this world who are alive now," said Aristarchus, "it is impacting all the spiritual realms above the earth too. This is incredible!"

Paul looked at each of the men with him. Then he knelt in front of them.

"Come, my dear brothers, let us pray together. I want to pray for you right now," said Paul.

The three men knelt on the floor alongside Paul, who lifted his hands heavenwards. Eyes open, he looked upwards with a serene expression.

"For this reason, I kneel before the Father, from whom every family in heaven and on earth derives its name. I pray that out of his glorious riches he may strengthen you with power through his Spirit in your inner being, so that Christ may dwell in your hearts through faith. And I pray that you, being rooted and established in love, may have power, together with all the Lord's holy people, to grasp how wide and long and high and deep is the love of Christ, and to know this love that surpasses knowledge, that you may be filled to the measure of all the fullness of God."[46]

As Paul prayed, he stood and placed a gentle hand on each of them, one after another.

"Now to him who is able to do immeasurably more than all we ask or imagine, according to his power that is at work within us, to him be glory in the assembly and in Christ Jesus throughout all generations, for ever and ever! Amen."[47]

⁂

The writing continued over the next two days. Paul had obviously been thinking and praying about what he was saying for quite some time, and he was in a flow of revelation from God. He began again,

"As a prisoner for the Lord, then, I urge you to live a life worthy of the calling you have received. Be completely humble and gentle; be patient, bearing with one another in love. Make every effort to

CHAPTER VII

keep the unity of the Spirit through the bond of peace. There is one body and one Spirit, just as you were called to one hope when you were called; one Lord, one faith, one baptism; one God and Father of all, who is over all and through all and in all."[48]

Titus was taking turns with Tychicus, helping with the writing. He raised his hand as if he were in a classroom.

"Can you repeat the last bit, Paul? I want to make sure I got the order right," said Titus. "I understand you are talking about God as being one. But I am not sure I understand how God is one yet there is one Spirit, one Lord and one Father. This sounds like three gods to me. How can God be one, yet also we experience him as three distinct persons?"

"This is one of the great mysteries of God," answered Paul. "What I know is this. He is eternal and unchanging, and he has revealed himself to us as the Father of the Lord Jesus. Jesus is distinct from the Father yet completely one with the Father. The Holy Spirit is his Spirit and together, the three are one."

Titus listened, nodded, and then said,

"Do you want me to write it down in the letter?"

"No," said Paul, "I think we need more revelation in explaining this. I somehow think others in the days to come will receive more insight and understanding from God on this. For now, we speak what we see and what we hear. Our experience of God is he is a Father to us and to Jesus. Jesus, his son, is fully God, the exact representation of God, the image of the invisible God, the firstborn over all creation. God was pleased to have all his fullness dwell in him, so he is also fully man, in human flesh. We are in Jesus, and he is in the Father. We also experience his Spirit within us and around us, speaking truth to our hearts. This is indeed a great mystery.

"Let us get back to the letter," said Paul.

Paul talked about the gifts God had given to his children and how those gifts and ministries would build and establish the community of believers. Paul went on to share how to live as sons of God in God's way.

"So, I tell you this, and insist on it in the Lord, that you must no longer live as the Gentiles do, in the futility of their thinking. They are darkened in their understanding and separated from the life of God because of the ignorance that is in them due to the hardening of their hearts. Having lost all sensitivity, they have given themselves over to sensuality so as to indulge in every kind of impurity, and they are full of greed."[49]

"When I hear you say this," said Aristarchus, "I remember so clearly how dark my life was before I met Jesus. I did not realise how blind I was. I followed all the usual things we Greeks did. My heart was so hard and insensitive."

"We were all like that, Aristarchus," added Titus. "I know what Paul means."

"When I was younger, I left Thessalonica," continued Aristarchus, "and I went to Corinth so I could go to the great temple up on the acropolis like everyone else. I spent money on those women in hope of getting some blessing from the goddess Aphrodite. All I got was the pox. I was so lost."

Titus sniggered.

"That will teach you," said Titus. "Have you heard the joke they tell about the sea captain who went up to the women on the

CHAPTER VII

acropolis?"

"No, don't." said Tychicus. "It's really funny, but it's filthy!" He started to laugh, and Titus continued with the joke. "It's about the prostitute with the really big—"

Paul interrupted them.

"Okay, stop right now. You boys, that will do. Come on now; let's get on with this."

Titus was still giggling and nudging Tychicus. But Paul gave them a look and continued,

"This is not the way of life you learned when you heard about Christ and were taught in him in accordance with the truth that is in Jesus. You were taught, with regard to your former way of life, to put off your old self, which is being corrupted by its deceitful desires; to be made new in the attitude of your minds; and to put on the new self, created to be like God in true righteousness and holiness."[50]

As Paul's words of life flowed, the three young friends of Paul stopped laughing. They realised they had gone too far in their banter. Paul continued,

"Do not let any unwholesome talk come out of your mouths, but only what is helpful for building others up according to their needs, that it may benefit those who listen. And do not grieve the Holy Spirit of God, with whom you were sealed for the day of redemption. Get rid of all bitterness, rage, and anger, brawling and slander, along with every form of malice. Be kind and compassionate to one another, forgiving each other, just as in Christ, God forgave you. Follow God's example, therefore, as dearly loved children and walk in the way of love, just as Christ loved us and gave himself up for us as a fragrant offering and sacrifice to God. But among you there must not be even a hint of sexual immorality, or any kind of impurity, or greed, because these are improper for God's holy people. Nor should there be obscenity, foolish talk, or coarse joking, which are out of place, but rather thanksgiving."[51]

Titus put down his stylus.

"I'm sorry, Paul, I really am. I did not mean to be rude. It is so easy to slip back into the old mindset, the old way of life," he said.

The three friends looked embarrassed and awkward. Paul went on,

"I am not trying to shame you. This is to say how it is and show how we are now free to live. Let's continue.

"For you were once darkness, but now you are light in the Lord. Live as children of light, for the fruit of the light consists in all goodness, righteousness, and truth. Find out what pleases the Lord. Have nothing to do with the fruitless deeds of darkness, but rather expose them. It is shameful even to mention what the disobedient do in secret. But everything exposed by the light becomes visible and everything that is illuminated becomes a light. This is why it is said, 'Wake up, sleeper, rise from the dead, and Christ will shine on you.'

"Be careful, then, how you live, not as unwise but as wise, making the most of every opportunity, because the days are evil. Therefore, do not be foolish, but understand what the Lord's will is. Do not get drunk on wine, which leads to debauchery. Instead, be filled with the Spirit, speaking to one another with psalms, hymns, and songs from the Spirit. Sing and make music from your heart to the Lord, always giving thanks to God the Father for everything, in the name of our Lord Jesus Christ."[52]

There was still a feeling of awkwardness in the room. So, Paul said,

CHAPTER VII

"Put the pen down a moment. I am not judging you. We all have these moments, boys, when our old life re-emerges."

Paul looked at them with understanding and affection in his eyes.

"The good we want to do we don't do and the wrong we don't want to do, we do. I don't know if you remember I wrote this in my letter to the Romans. I still find myself slipping back into this old way of thinking and behaving.

"But thank God, he delivers us through our Lord Jesus Christ! There is no condemnation for us because we are in Christ. Through Christ Jesus, the law of the Spirit of life has set us free from the law of sin and death.

"Titus, let me have a look at what you have written." Paul held the manuscript close to his eyes. "Here it is, read it back to me please, Titus."

Titus took the manuscript and read aloud what Paul had written,

"Put off your old self, which is being corrupted by its deceitful desires; and be made new in the attitude of your minds; and to put on the new self, created to be like God in true righteousness and holiness."

"Let's have a break for a while," said Paul.

Philip and his wife had arrived a few minutes before bringing with them a basket of food for everyone. As usual, the guard who was seldom seen mysteriously reappeared when the food arrived. The smell of freshly baked bread and grilled fish filled the room. Philip's wife had anticipated the guard would be there and invited him to join them in the meal.

He looked surprised at her invitation but agreed. After he thanked them, he said to Philip,

"Can I ask a question, sir?"

"Of course," said Philip. "What is your question?"

"I have been watching you and listening to you; the way you talk to each other. I've watched you and your wife," he said pointing to Philip.

"I've seen how you both come here bringing food, but more than this, I've never seen a couple behave like you two. You seem to really love each other. I have never seen you strike her or heard you shout at her. You seem to not only love each other but respect each other. You let her speak, and she does not need to ask your permission first. I'm amazed. I have never seen people behave like this before. Why do you do this?"

Philip looked at his wife who smiled at him. She turned to the guard and said,

"It's because of what Jesus has done for us.

"We love each other and delight to submit to each other as equals. We do this with joy. I love my husband and I know he loves me and am happy to follow his lead in our marriage because I see him following Jesus. It is not difficult doing this when he is laying down his life for me like Jesus did. I respect him. This is how we all try to behave in our community of believers."

Philip smiled at the guard.

"Maybe you could come to one of our gatherings and you can meet more of us."

After the meal was eaten, Philip and his wife left Paul to lay down on his mat and rest. The summer heat was beginning to build, and

CHAPTER VII

the afternoons were hot leaving the cell stuffy. Soon, the room was full of snoring men.

Paul woke thinking about the conversation between the guard and Philip's wife, and he knew what he needed to write next. He looked at the sleeping men. One by one, they stirred and readied themselves to continue the work.

"I want to continue. I have been thinking about how we relate to each other when we are in Christ," Paul said.

"I'm ready when you are," said Tychicus.

"Submit to one another out of reverence for Christ," said Paul. "Wives, submit yourselves to your own husbands as you do to the Lord. For the husband is the head of the wife as Christ is the head of the assembly, his body, of which he is the Saviour. Now as the gathered community of believers submits to Christ, so also wives should submit to their husbands in everything."[53]

"This is what Philip and his wife were explaining to the guard earlier," said Paul. Then he continued his line of thought.

"Husbands, love your wives, just as Christ loved the assembly of believers and gave himself up for us to make us holy, cleansing us by the washing with water through the word, and to present us to himself as a radiant people without stain or wrinkle or any other blemish, but holy and blameless. In this same way, husbands ought to love their wives as their own bodies. He who loves his wife loves himself."[54]

Paul continued writing practical advice for married couples, children, parents, and also for slaves and masters. He knew some of his friends had formerly been slaves and many in the scattered communities of believers were still slaves. They had to suffer the humiliation

THE STORY OF PAUL III

and struggles of slavery and were not free. He was grateful for these three companions who were with him, willingly supporting him and encouraging him. He knew they ran great personal risk to walk with him on his journey. He thought of Lucas in Jerusalem with Peter, Timothy in Ephesus, Lydia in Philippi and so many others.

Paul announced they had finished for the day and the three men went back to their lodgings in the city. Alone with his thoughts, Paul knew he was nearly finished with the letter. He had been in this confined situation for almost two years. He wondered how much longer he would be in the cell. It was not too difficult. He had food and a comfortable mattress. He was free to write and receive visitors, but he was not free to leave.

During the night, Paul awoke to loud voices and a disturbance. He stood to look out his small window. The courtyard was full of soldiers and slaves carrying goods into the palace yard.

At first light, as soon as his guard appeared, Paul asked what was going on.

"Felix has been replaced as governor of the province," the guard said excitedly. "An imperial galley arrived during the night with the new governor, a detachment of soldiers and various officials and bureaucrats from Rome. I heard a rumour this morning that Felix doesn't know yet as he is in Jerusalem. He won't be happy about this," laughed the guard.

"Who is the new governor?" asked Paul.

"Someone called Porcius Festus. I've never heard of him. He has gone to the governor's residence and will go to Jerusalem in a couple of days to break the news to Felix. He has also brought a cohort of soldiers with him to beef up the numbers as things are getting quite

CHAPTER VII

tense in Jerusalem and in the province in general. The Zealots are getting bolder."

"Is that why there are many more soldiers here now?" asked Paul.

"Yes, apparently. And Herod Agrippa and his so-called wife are in Judea. They might have to move back here if the new governor wants the palace at Herodium for himself."

"This is his palace, but he is never here. Why? Do you know?" asked Paul.

"Well, it's complicated, like everything else in the Herod family," answered the guard. "Marcus Julius Agrippa, who styles himself King Herod Agrippa II, is the great grandson of the last of the Jewish kings, King Herod the Great, who ruled over the whole of the province of Judaea before the Romans annexed Judea."

"Doesn't he have influence and power though?" asked Paul.

"In reality, he has little authority and no real power. His prestige comes from being a survivor and close friend of the last emperor, Claudius. Most of his relatives in the Herod dynasty died in mysterious circumstances or were deliberately murdered in family feuds. He and Claudius, however, were both survivors. Through political manoeuvring and fox-like cunning, which is a family trait, Agrippa has survived. Despite Claudius dying, or being killed, and the accession of the totally insane Nero, Agrippa has survived."

"But why do you call his wife 'so-called'?" asked Paul.

"It's easy. She is his sister," The guard sniggered. "Berenice, she calls herself. Her sister Drusilla is married to the outgoing governor, so the change won't please the Herod family."

"His sister," exclaimed Paul. "Are you sure?"

"If the rumours about their relationship and the graffiti on the walls of the brothels in Caesarea are anything to go by, it is more than a brotherly and sisterly one," replied the guard.

The guard having enjoyed passing on the gossip left. Paul watched the soldiers and activity in the courtyard for a while. He considered the implication of the news and decided he needed to finish writing his letter as soon as possible in case his circumstances suddenly changed. He expected Tychicus and maybe the others to come later in the morning.

He watched two of the soldiers who had taken up guard duty standing at the entry to the palace. They were dressed in full Roman military style with shiny breastplates, helmets, and greaves on their lower legs. On the belts around their waists hung the typical short broad sword. Oblong Roman shields rested up against the wall.

Tychicus arrived, along with Aristarchus and Titus who had also heard the news of the change of governor.

"I want to get on and finish the letter," said Paul. "There is change in the air and I feel a sense of urgency. So, let's begin."

Paul was still looking out into the courtyard as he spoke.

"Finally, be strong in the Lord and in his mighty power. Put on the full armour of God, so that you can take your stand against the devil's schemes. For our struggle is not against flesh and blood, but against the rulers, against the authorities, against the powers of this dark world and against the spiritual forces of evil in the heavenly realms."

He waited while Tychicus wrote, then continued,

"Therefore, put on the full armour of God, so that when the day

CHAPTER VII

of evil comes, you may be able to stand your ground, and after you have done everything, to stand. Stand firm then, with the belt of truth buckled around your waist, with the breastplate of righteousness in place, and with your feet fitted with the readiness that comes from the gospel of peace. In addition to all this, take up the shield of faith, with which you can extinguish all the flaming arrows of the evil one. Take the helmet of salvation and the sword of the Spirit, which is the word of God.

"And pray in the Spirit on all occasions with all kinds of prayers and requests. With this in mind, be alert and always keep on praying for all the Lord's people. Pray also for me, that whenever I speak, words may be given me so that I will fearlessly make known the mystery of the gospel, for which I am an ambassador in chains. Pray that I may declare it fearlessly, as I should."[55]

Paul asked Tychicus to reread what he had just said. When he finished, Paul was satisfied.

"Tychicus, I would really like you to carry this letter to our friends in the assemblies in Asia. How do you feel about this?" asked Paul.

"I would be happy to do this," said Tychicus. "I would also like to take a copy of Lucas' work about Jesus to them. Maybe if I took the overland route, I could visit Antioch and Galatia before arriving in Ephesus. Would that be a good plan?"

"An excellent plan. Titus, will you go with him? Somehow, I don't think I will be in prison much longer and I still hope to go to Rome. But, how and when, I am not sure. Aristarchus, would you be willing to stay with me? I think Lucas will be returning soon. I would appreciate you being with me at this time."

"There is no question in my mind," said Aristarchus. "I will stay with you and go with you even to Rome. I think we need to send a message to Lucas as soon as possible so he knows what we are thinking."

"Thank you, Ari," said Paul. "Can you send a message to Lucas for me? Now let me finish the letter."

Paul began again with his final thoughts.

"Tychicus, the dear brother and faithful servant in the Lord, will tell you everything, so that you also may know how I am and what I am doing. I am sending him to you for this purpose, that you may know how we are, and that he may encourage you. Peace to the brothers and sisters, and love with faith from God the Father and the Lord Jesus Christ. Grace to all who love our Lord Jesus Christ with an undying love."[56]

CHAPTER VIII

The next morning, the guard appeared at the door of Paul's cell somewhat agitated.

"The new governor is making his mark already," said the guard. "It seems Felix has fallen out of favour and Festus is here to clear up the mess. There is a big shake up going on, and new officers in charge now. It looks like I will be relieved of my duties and posted elsewhere. I have had to report on you too. Festus wants to know who you are and why you are here."

"When are you being replaced?" asked Paul.

"Festus is going to Jerusalem in a day or two to kick Felix out and I imagine I will go soon after. You never know, you might be released... or maybe not. It might be worse for you," said the guard.

The guard left and within an hour, a group of Paul's friends came to see him. They had all heard the news and were concerned for Paul's situation.

"It may be good news," said Philip. "Perhaps this is God's intervention. Whatever is going on with the Romans, we need to be prepared."

"I have finished the letter I have been writing and Tychicus will take it to Asia. Titus will go with him but may stop at various places on the way to encourage the believers. I have also sent for Lucas to return. Other than this, I don't know what else we can do."

"I would like to have a copy of your letter to keep here," said Philip. "Perhaps we can get a group of amanuenses together to copy the manuscripts of this new letter and Lucas' account."

"I can organise this," said Tychicus. "And I agree, time is of the essence."

∧∧∧∨∨∨∧∧

Three days after arriving in Caesarea, Festus left for Jerusalem. Lucas returned the same day.

When they all met, Lucas said,

"I passed a large group of Romans heading for Jerusalem on my way down here. Festus looks a lot more disciplined than Felix. He was in full armour, obviously trying to make an impression."

"Well, it won't be long before things change around here. How was your time with Peter?" asked Paul.

"Excellent," said Lucas. "I have so much more material for my second book and a much clearer picture of the events that unfolded in the early years following the resurrection here in Jerusalem and Judea. I have made notes. Now I need time to put them together."

"Where is Peter now?" asked Paul.

"He has gone to Galilee. He has family there he wants to see. He talked also of going to Galatia, Cappadocia, Bithynia, and even Pontus. He has been there before and wants to see the brothers there again. He wrote to them a while ago. He plans to take John Mark with him if he does go," said Lucas.

CHAPTER VIII

Lucas went back to Theophilus' house to check on the progress of the copying of the various manuscripts. He was delighted with the copying of his first book and eager for a copy to be sent to Ephesus. Tychicus had done an excellent job in organising the work. It occurred to Lucas centres of copying were needed in most of the communities as more of Paul's letters and the accounts of the life of Jesus began to circulate.

As he sat in the scriptorium, Lucas wondered about all the material he had collected for his sequel. He was looking through the various sheets when his host knocked on the side of the doorframe.

"May I come in, Luke? I don't want to disturb you if you are busy," said Theophilus.

"No, please come in, Theo. Sit with me, I have some things I could do with some advice on," said Lucas.

"What things?" asked Theophilus.

"Well, it's all this material I have collected for my second book. I am beginning to fit it all together, but it ends abruptly with Paul's arrest and being here in custody in Caesarea for two years. I really don't think it is finished yet. I don't know how it will end though."

"Perhaps the next part will be about Paul's release," said Theophilus. "I'm sure the new governor won't keep him here much longer. There is no point. The Jewish authorities have had two years to make a charge against him and they have not been able to do anything. As soon as he sees this is the case, I'm hopeful he will release Paul. Has Paul mentioned what he wants to do next?"

"He talks all the time about wanting to take the message to the west, to Rome, to Spain even," said Lucas. "Also, he thinks a lot about Timothy and the assemblies in Greece, Asia, and Macedonia.

I think it is all in Father's hands."

"Whatever you decide to do, you are welcome to leave all your manuscripts here with me and in due time you can come back and finish the work when you have a clearer idea. You may not want to be carrying a great pile of papyrus around with you when Paul sets off on his travels again. You know you are always welcome here, Luke."

"Thank you. At least I know they would be safe," added Lucas.

※

Later the same week, Zacchaeus came from Jerusalem. He had news and gathered the leaders all together in Paul's cell. The room was crowded as they listened to his report.

"You all know I have contacts within the Sanhedrin in Jerusalem. My friends there came to me with this news. Apparently, as soon as they could, the chief priests and the Jewish leaders went to Festus with a myriad of things but also this. They presented charges against Paul, and they have requested Festus, as a 'favour' to them, have Paul transferred to Jerusalem. My friend tells me they are preparing an ambush to kill him along the way."

"This is serious," said Philip. "How can we prevent this?"

"We don't need to," said Zacchaeus. "Festus told them Paul is being held at Caesarea, and Festus himself is coming here soon. He told them some of their leaders must come with him, and if the man has done anything wrong, they can press charges against him here."

Theophilus' house became a hive of activity as Philip, assisted by Tychicus, gathered a team of amanuenses to copy the manuscripts. One group worked on Paul's letter in the scriptorium and another

CHAPTER VIII

group worked on Lucas' manuscript which they were beginning to call the *good news*.

Within a week, all the work was finished and Tychicus and Titus were ready to head north with the copied manuscripts. They decided to take the overland route rather than go by sea taking the pack horse originally given to Lucas by Lysias. They would head for Antioch first, then go through Galatia to Asia. They embraced Paul, Lucas, and Aristarchus before departing and promised to send news as soon as they arrived at their destinations.

Everything went quiet for a few days after Tychicus and Titus left. Then late one evening, soldiers arrived from Jerusalem and quickly word spread of Porcius Festus' return from Jerusalem. Paul's guard arrived early in the morning.

"Festus is back," he said, "and he has convened a court to deal with a few outstanding cases. You are on the slate, so get yourself ready. They will send guards to take you to the court."

"Can you send a message to Lucas to let him know?" asked Paul.

The guard looked at him inquisitively and Paul knew there was a price to pay for this request.

"I am sure Philip's wife will be bringing food today," said Paul with a grin.

While they were talking, two armed guards entered the courtyard with an officer.

"Where is the prisoner Paul of Tarsus?" The officer looked around as Paul's guard led him out of his cell.

"I am he," said Paul.

"You are commanded to appear before his Excellency Porcius

Festus at the governor's residence immediately. Come with us."

The two guards took Paul and bound his hands, then led him roughly out of the courtyard.

As he was being marched through the city to the governor's residence, Paul caught sight of his guard scuttling ahead and making for Theophilus' house where Lucas was staying. Once escorted into the residence, Paul was made to wait in a hallway while the officer reported his arrival to the governor. He returned after about an hour and said,

"It's you, now. Come with me."

They entered the audience chamber, and the guard announced,

"The prisoner, Paul of Tarsus, Your Excellency."

Paul entered and looked around. Festus was seated on a raised dais at the end of the hall surrounded by officials and a scribe at a desk. To his left were a group of Jews who had come down from Jerusalem. To the right behind a wooden rail were a crowd of people who were obviously waiting for a case of someone they knew. He spotted Lucas and Theophilus edging through the crowd to the front.

Festus looked curiously at Paul.

"I understand you are a Roman citizen by birth. Is that correct?" he asked.

"Indeed, Your Excellency, from the noble city of Tarsus in Cilicia," answered Paul.

"Why is he bound?" asked Festus. "That is no way to treat a Roman citizen. Officer, untie him. You, Paul, come closer so I can see you properly."

CHAPTER VIII

After Paul was unbound, he stepped forward making a point of rubbing his wrists. Festus looked closely at him, then turned to the group of Jews waiting to present their charges. He addressed them.

"State your accusations and the evidence to back them up and don't take all day about it."

The Jewish religious leaders presented a list of serious charges against Paul, but they had no more evidence two years after the fact than they had previously. It was a matter of Paul's word versus theirs.

Lucas whispered to Theophilus,

"There are rumours they never worked on gathering any real evidence because they always intended to assassinate Paul. I wonder if Festus knows this?"

As Paul listened to the charges, he remembered how Jesus appeared to him two years before when he was first arrested in Jerusalem and had said, 'Take courage! As you have testified about me in Jerusalem, so you must also testify in Rome.' Paul knew he would never get a fair trial in Jerusalem and began thinking about appealing to Caesar, a right granted to Roman citizens. He knew 'Appealing to Caesar' was rarely done, but it was allowed by law.

When the Jewish leaders concluded their accusations, Festus turned to Paul and instructed him to make his defence.

"I have done nothing wrong against the Jewish law or against the temple or against Caesar," said Paul.

Festus listened and wishing to ingratiate himself with the Jewish authorities said to Paul,

"Are you willing to go up to Jerusalem and stand trial before me in the city on these charges?"

"I am standing right now before Caesar's court, where I ought to be tried. I have not done any wrong to the Jews, as you yourself well know. If, however, I am guilty of doing anything deserving death, I do not refuse to die. But if the charges brought against me by these Jews are not true, no one has the right to hand me over to them."

Paul paused and looked intently at Festus.

"Therefore, I appeal to Caesar."

There was a stunned silence in the hall, then murmurings among all the various groups. To go to Rome was expensive and rarely did the emperor overturn a previous decision. However, in this case, no decision had been made. Quite new at his post, Festus conferred with his officials. They told him he would need to write a letter of explanation to Caesar. Festus had no choice but to grant Paul's request. He did not want to portray himself as incompetent but found himself at a loss for words. Finally turning back to the assembly gathered in the hall, he declared.

"You have appealed to Caesar. To Caesar you will go!"[57]

CHAPTER IX

Paul was led out of the audience chamber and instead of being taken back to his cell in Agrippa's palace, he was placed in one of the underground dungeons in the governor's residence. And there he remained. He was allowed to have food sent to him, but the guards were not as amenable as the one who had been responsible for him in Agrippa's palace. When the food was delivered to his cell, most of it had been stolen and what was left was scraps. The cell was dark and damp. There was a slop bucket, which no one came to empty. Within a short time, Paul became lousy, hungry, dirty, and discouraged.

∿∿∿

Meanwhile, to Festus' great delight, Agrippa II, and his sister, Berenice came to pay a state visit to meet the new governor in Caesarea. They moved back into their palace and entertained him with a lavish display of opulence and luxury. There were banquets and parties attended by many of the local wealthy and influential inhabitants of the city. The dinners went late into the night and vast quantities of food and wine were consumed. Paul was not at the forefront of Festus' mind. None of Paul's friends were able to gain access to him in the dreadful cell in the bowels of the governor's residence.

After a couple of weeks of festivities, Festus' head began to clear. As he sobered, he decided to explain to Agrippa and Berenice how he had inherited the messy case of Paul from Felix.

"There is a man here whom Felix left as a prisoner. When I went to Jerusalem, the chief priests and the elders of the Jews brought charges against him and demanded he be condemned on the spot," said Festus.

"I told them it is not the Roman custom to hand over anyone before they have faced their accusers and have had an opportunity to defend themselves against the charges.

"I didn't delay the case. Instead, I convened the court the next day and ordered the man to be brought in. When his accusers got up to speak, they did not charge him with any of the crimes I had expected. They merely had points of dispute with him about their own religion and about a dead man named Jesus who this man Paul claimed was alive. I asked if he would be willing to go to Jerusalem and stand trial there on these charges. But then he made his appeal to be held over for the Emperor's decision. As a Roman citizen, he has the right.

"I am really at a loss to know what to do with him," Festus explained.

"I have never had to investigate religious matters before. They told me in Rome this would be a difficult governorship as you Jews are notoriously obtuse and argumentative."

Agrippa grinned, nodding sympathetically, but managed to sneak a wink at Berenice.

CHAPTER IX

"How can I help?" Agrippa attempted to sound concerned.

"I think the evidence against the man is weak," said Festus. "But when the prisoner appealed for the Emperor's decision, I ordered him to be held until I can send him to Caesar."

"This sounds unusual," said Agrippa. "I have heard about these people who are followers of the rabbi from Nazareth. He was crucified by one of your predecessors over thirty years ago. But quickly a story was spread about him coming back from the dead. You know how simple and feeble-minded people love these fantasies. I am aware there are many in Judea who believe this nonsense. It has spread quite widely. I am told even to Rome itself. Isn't that so, Berenice?"

"Yes, so I hear. I have never met any of these people. It might be entertaining to hear him, darling. I love a good ghost story." purred Berenice in Agrippa's ear.

Festus was delighted and relieved to have someone who might be able to help him resolve the case. As a result, the next day Paul was brought before the authorities.

When Paul was led into the audience chamber to await the arrival of the officials, he was relieved to see a large group of his friends in the public area waving and shouting greetings to him.

The doors opened and Festus entered followed by Agrippa and Berenice with great pomp. Behind them, high-ranking military officers and prominent men of the city followed. Paul stood before them chained hand and foot.

For those who were seeing him for the first time, they saw a short man, whose age was difficult to determine. His hair thin and lank, his balding head scarred. Age lines framed the eyes of his pale face. Two weeks of incarceration in a dark cell had leached the tan of his travels out of his skin turning it into a pallid paste that highlighted the scars of frequent beatings. His nose was bent and hooked having appeared to have been broken numerous times.

The prisoner's eyes were red like flames as he struggled to focus on the people in front of him. For years, Paul had suffered with eye infections and poor eyesight. Now, after being kept in a dark cell, they burned and stung in the bright light of the audience chamber. The fetid stink of prison clung to his filthy tunic, invading the space of those nearby. One of the guards wrinkled his nose and shifted sideways to distance himself from the miasma wafting around him.

Paul stood slightly stooped and raised his head to look up at the assembled group of dignitaries arrayed before him like classical Greek actors in the theatre of his hometown, Tarsus. In the centre, occupying the seat of honour, sat King Agrippa II, Marcus Julius Agrippa to be precise. Next to him sat his sister Julia Berenice draped across the chair beside her brother, leaning towards him in a less than sisterly way.

Alongside these two, dressed in a toga, sat the newly appointed Roman governor of the province, Porcius Festus.

Festus addressed the gathered group of dignitaries and officials.

"King Agrippa, and all who are present with us, you see this man."

"I can see him and smell him from here," said Berenice loud enough for everyone to hear.

Agrippa shot her a glance that he hoped would silence her. Instead, she feigned a sulky smirk. Laughter ripped around the hall to the annoyance of Festus, who called for silence before he continued.

"The whole Jewish community has petitioned me about him in

CHAPTER IX

Jerusalem and here in Caesarea, demanding he ought not live any longer. I found he has done nothing deserving of death. But because he made his appeal to the Emperor, I decided to send him to Rome though I have nothing definitive to write to his majesty about him. Therefore, I have brought him before all of you, and especially before you, King Agrippa, so that as a result of this investigation, I may have something to write. For I think it is unreasonable to send a prisoner on to Rome without specifying the charges against him."

"You have permission to speak for yourself." Agrippa then said to Paul.

Every eye in the great audience hall turned and looked at the diminutive figure standing in chains in the centre. In reality, before these gathered dignitaries stood a towering spiritual giant of a man, Paul the Apostle, Saul of Tarsus, the great revealer of truth, one of the greatest minds the world had known.

This was perhaps his greatest moment so far with the most significant audience Paul had ever addressed. He was about to tell them his story in his own words. Every thought would be crafted in his brilliant mind before being uttered. Every word carefully chosen. Every pause pregnant with meaning. Every gesture adding effect. His voice, his tone, his passion would resonate through every sentence.

Paul struggled to raise his manacled hand to indicate he was about to begin his defence. The whole hall fell silent. Even Berenice stopped whispering to Agrippa and looked at Paul.

"King Agrippa," began Paul, slightly bowing before the king, "I consider myself fortunate to stand before you today as I make my defence against all the accusations of the Jews, and especially so because you are well acquainted with all the Jewish customs and controversies. Therefore, I beg you to listen to me patiently.

"The Jewish people all know the way I have lived ever since I was a child, from the beginning of my life in my own country and also in Jerusalem. They have known me for a long time and can testify, if they are willing, that I conformed to the strictest sect of our religion, living as a Pharisee. And now it is because of my hope in what God has promised our ancestors that I am on trial today. This is the promise our twelve tribes are hoping to see fulfilled as they earnestly serve God day and night. King Agrippa, it is because of this hope that these Jews are accusing me."

Paul deliberately referenced the twelve tribes of Israel as he knew Agrippa would connect with this historical reference rather than just refer to the Jews. Paul's knowledge of rhetoric served him well in situations like this as he asked a rhetorical question.

"Why should any of you consider it incredible that God raises the dead?"

This underlined his credentials as a Pharisee and without attempting to answer the question, he went on to explain his own personal response to the report of Jesus being resurrected.

"I was convinced that I ought to do all that was possible to oppose the name of Jesus of Nazareth. And it is just what I did in Jerusalem. On the authority of the chief priests, I put many of Jesus' followers in prison, and when they were put to death, I cast my vote against them. Many a time I went from one synagogue to another to have them punished, and I tried to force them to blaspheme. I was so obsessed with persecuting them that I even hunted them down in foreign cities.

"On one of these journeys, I was going to Damascus with the

CHAPTER IX

authority and commission of the chief priests. About noon, O King, I was on the road and I saw a light from heaven, brighter than the sun, blazing around me and my companions. We all fell to the ground, and I heard a voice saying to me in Aramaic, 'Saul, Saul, why do you persecute me? It is hard for you to kick against the goads.'"

"I bet he had been drinking," said Berenice loudly hoping to raise a laugh. But no one in the hall laughed; every eye was fixed on Paul.

Paul ignored her and continued.

"Then I asked, 'Who are you, Lord?'

"'I am Jesus, whom you are persecuting,' the Lord replied. 'Now get up and stand on your feet. I have appeared to you to appoint you as a servant and a witness of what you have seen and will see of me. I will rescue you from your own people and from the Gentiles. I am sending you to them to open their eyes and turn them from darkness to light, and from the power of Satan to God, so that they may receive forgiveness of sins and a place among those who are sanctified by faith in me.'

"So then, King Agrippa, I was not disobedient to the vision from heaven. First to those in Damascus, then to those in Jerusalem and in all Judea, and then to the Gentiles, I preached that they should repent and turn to God and demonstrate their repentance by their deeds. That is why some Jews seized me in the temple courts and tried to kill me.

"But God has helped me to this day. So, I stand here and testify to small and great alike. I am saying nothing beyond what the prophets and Moses said would happen, that the Messiah would suffer and, as the first to rise from the dead, would bring the message of light to his own people and to the Gentiles."

At this point, Festus interrupted Paul's defence.

"You are out of your mind, Paul!" he shouted. "Your great learning is driving you insane."

"I am not insane, most excellent Festus," Paul replied. "What I am saying is true and reasonable. The king is familiar with these things, and I can speak freely to him. This was not done in a corner, and I am convinced that none of this has escaped his notice. King Agrippa, do you believe the prophets? I know you do."

Berenice leaned over and whispered something to him. Then Agrippa said to Paul,

"Do you think that in such a short time you can persuade me to be a Christian?"

Paul replied, "Short time or long, I pray to God that not only you but all who are listening to me today may become what I am, except for these chains." A snigger went through the watching crowd.

The king rose, and with him the governor and Berenice and those sitting with them. As they left the room, Festus said,

"This man has done nothing that deserves death or imprisonment."

Agrippa agreed. To Festus, he said, "This man could have been set free if he had not appealed to Caesar."[58]

Paul was taken back to his cell. The leaders of the community of believers in Caesarea petitioned Festus for Paul to be released to house arrest while they awaited his departure to Rome.

Festus agreed to meet their representatives, and Cornelius and Theophilus presented themselves to the governor.

CHAPTER IX

Festus pointed out whilst Paul was technically not a convicted prisoner, he still needed to be taken to Rome under guard because he appealed to the emperor. Then he agreed Paul could be held at Theophilus' house until his departure.

"I have arranged his passage to Rome be supervised by a centurion of the Imperial Regiment," said Festus. "He will carry a letter of explanation to present to the emperor on his arrival in Rome. The centurion will make the arrangements. If Paul disappears before a ship can be organised, I will hold you both personally responsible and it will be you two who go to Rome. Is that clear?" Before either could respond, Festus continued. "Now get out of my sight I want to hear no more about this case or this man Paul."

CHAPTER X

After two years of little happening, things rapidly changed. A messenger arrived at Theophilus' house two days later with a document. Theophilus took it and read it aloud to Lucas, Aristarchus, and Paul.

"The citizen known as Paul of Tarsus is commanded to report to the governor's residence tomorrow morning at first light. You will identify yourself to the Centurion Julius of the Imperial Regiment in whose custody you will be held until you are delivered by him personally to the official in Rome at the Imperial Palace who handles all legal appeals. Any attempt to escape or abscond at any point will be taken as an admission of guilt and on recapture you will face the severest consequences appropriate to your alleged crimes. You will be responsible for all your own expenses throughout. You may, if you wish, be accompanied by up to two companions who will travel at their own expense. Signed by order of his excellency, Governor of the Province of Judea, Porcius Festus."

"I wonder what my alleged crimes are?" said Paul. "Probably the trumped-up charges which were read at my latest hearing."

"Now listen to us, Paul," said Aristarchus. "Lucas and I have talked, and we are both in agreement. We are coming with you to Rome. We want no argument. It's a done deal. Someone needs to

CHAPTER X

carry your bags and look after the money."

"And I am going to make sure you stay healthy too," said Lucas.

Paul looked at them both. His face said he was greatly relieved.

As instructed, Paul reported to the governor's residence at first light accompanied by his two companions. From there, they were escorted to the dock down at the harbour. A crowd of people were milling around, including several believers from the community in the city. Philip and his family, Theophilus, Zacchaeus and Cornelius gathered around the three men and embraced them. Bundles of food were added to their baggage. Sailors and slaves were loading cargo onto the large merchant ship.

"Get back, you people," barked the centurion as he marched over to Paul. "Move out of my way. Which of you is the prisoner Paul of Tarsus?"

"This is Paul, and may I remind you he is a Roman citizen and deserves the respect due a citizen," said a serious and authoritative Cornelius to the centurion. Julius was half his age and recognised him straight away.

"Are you with this man, sir?" he asked. "I had no idea. My apologies."

"I believe in the same God as he does, but I am not accompanying him to Rome," said Cornelius. "These two men are going with him. None of them are prisoners and need to be treated with respect as passengers. Both are Greeks, and this man, Lucas, is a physician. Paul is to arrive in Rome in good physical condition. Is that clear to you?"

"Perfectly, sir," said Julius to Cornelius.

THE STORY OF PAUL III

Among the crowd were a group of bedraggled and depressed looking men. They were all chained together. There must have been about seventy of them. They were being herded together towards the gang plank.

"Who are these men?" asked Cornelius.

"They are all slaves," replied Julius. "A mixture of criminals destined for glory in the arenas of Rome. The healthier ones will probably be sold in the slave market. I'm responsible to get as many of them alive to Rome as I can."

Along with the prisoners were ten soldiers of the Imperial Regiment under Julius' command.

"We are awaiting another passenger and cannot leave until he arrives," said Julius to Cornelius. "He should be here soon. He arrived yesterday and is probably sleeping off last night's drinking."

"Who is it?" asked Cornelius.

"A military tribune removed from his post in the reshuffle which has been going on since Governor Festus arrived, sir. He has been up in Galilee for some time but hasn't done a good job. He hasn't the stomach for crucifying insurrectionists and zealots apparently." As Julius said this, a clattering of horses' hooves announced the arrival of the last passenger.

The urbane tribune jumped down from his horse and demanded to know where Julius was.

"I presume you are Tribune Claudius Lysias?" asked Julius as the officer walked towards him.

"You only just made it, sir. We depart shortly," said Julius.

"Oh! For the love of Jupiter, is that the ship? It's a merchantman.

CHAPTER X

I thought it would at least be a bireme."

Lucas immediately recognised Lysias. Grinning widely, he walked up to him.

"Well! Well! Well! I'd recognise that voice anywhere," said Lucas.

Lysias spun around; his mouth opened in surprise.

"Luke! What for the love of Zeus are you doing here?" he grasped Lucas by his forearms in the Roman fashion and then looked around.

"Oh, no. Not him too," he said pointing at Paul. "I thought he was dead. The last I heard he was locked up in some dungeon somewhere. I presumed he was dead."

"We have lots to tell you, my friend, and we will have the time to do it as we are on this boat bound for Rome also," said Lucas.

A messenger arrived from the governor with a large satchel.

"This is from the Governor Porcius Festus," whispered the man. "It contains letters for the emperor concerning the citizen Paul and also concerning the Tribune Claudius Lysias. There are a few reports and a letter you must guard with your life."

Julius looked concerned as he opened the satchel and checked its contents. Then he grinned and began to laugh.

"Oh, Yes. I see why," he said. "It's a letter to Festus' wife in Rome."

The messenger saluted and left.

They boarded the ship which had come from Adramyttium and was sailing along the coasts heading for the province of Asia. Winter was approaching and the weather was already beginning to change. They knew the journey could potentially be long and hazardous. As the ship put out to sea, the group of believers on the quay side began to sing and wave farewell to Paul, Aristarchus, and Lucas. The passengers and crew on deck were initially amused, and then became curious as they watched the affectionate farewell.

The ship sailed for one day up the coast to Sidon and put into the port to collect more cargo. Paul asked Julius if he might go ashore to greet his friends in the city. To everyone's amazement, he granted Paul's request.

"There is something about this man," said Paul to Lucas and Aristarchus. "He has granted us favour."

"Even Lysias has stopped pretending to be a haughty officer," said Lucas. "He is quite vulnerable and depressed. He wonders what is in store for him when he gets to Rome. I think it is going to be an interesting voyage."

"What do you mean *interesting*?" asked Aristarchus. "I knew a slave once from Britannia who used that word all the time."

From there they put out to sea again and passed to the lee of Cyprus because the winds were against them. After sailing across the open sea off the coast of Cilicia and Pamphylia, they landed at Myra in Lycia. This was as far as the ship was going, so the centurion had to find another ship. He found an Alexandrian ship sailing for Italy and they were all put onboard this new ship.

The weather was against them, and they made slow headway for many days and had difficulty arriving off Cnidus. The wind did not allow them to hold their course, so they sailed to the lee of Crete, opposite Salomne. Half the ship's company was seasick. Lucas was busy trying to help people. The prisoners below deck were in appalling conditions and a few had already died. Their bodies were tossed overboard by the crew.

CHAPTER X

"Receive these gifts, great Poseidon, and let us all live," they cried out as the corpses splashed into the water.

The ship moved slowly along the coast with great difficulty and finally came to a place called Fair Havens, near the town of Lasea where they put in for shelter. Much time had been lost. It was after the Jewish Day of Atonement and late in the year when sailing became more dangerous.

"I can see our voyage is going to be disastrous," said Paul to the captain, "and bring great loss to ship and cargo, and to our own lives. I urge you to stay here."

"Don't listen to him. What does he know?" said the owner of the ship to the captain. "Unlike this fool, you know what we are doing. I say we put out to sea and hold our course steady westwards."

Julius, the centurion, was in a quandary. Instead of listening to Paul, he followed the advice of the owner and the captain since the harbour was unsuitable to spend the winter in and the majority decided they should sail on.

"If we go now, we can make it to Phoenix and winter there. It's a good harbour, facing both southwest and northwest," said the captain.

A gentle south wind began to blow and seeing their opportunity, they weighed anchor and sailed along the coast of Crete. Before long, a seasonal wind of hurricane force, known as the Euroclydon by the Cretans, swept down from the island. Caught by the storm, the ship could not head into the wind. So, they gave way to it and were driven along passing to the lee of a small island called Cauda. As the situation rapidly deteriorated, everyone became terrified.

"Get the lifeboat," shouted the captain to one of the crew. "Secure it to the deck with ropes and try to pass the ropes under the keel from the bows to give added strength to hold the boat together."

In desperation, various attempts were made to secure the ship. Afraid of running aground on the sandbars off Syrtis, they lowered the sea anchor and let the ship be driven along. The boat took a violent battering from the storm and the next day they had to throw the cargo overboard. On the third day, they threw the ship's tackle overboard. Panic was stalking the ship.

Neither sun nor stars appeared for many days and the storm continued raging. They gave up all hope of being saved. All the people on the boat tried to snatch sleep when they could. Paul was curled up, soaking wet below deck, praying. Suddenly, an angel of the Lord stood beside him.

"Do not be afraid, Paul," said the angel. "You must stand trial before Caesar, and God has graciously given you the lives of all who sail with you."

In a brief lull, Paul staggered onto the deck and stood before the captain and crew. He told them what he had seen, and then added.

"You should have taken my advice not to sail from Crete, then you would have spared yourselves this damage and loss."

"Somebody shut him up," shouted the captain.

"I urge you to keep up your courage," continued Paul ignoring the captain. "Not one of you will be lost, only the ship will be destroyed. So, keep up your courage, men, for I have faith in God that it will happen just as he told me."

Fourteen nights after they left Crete, they were still being driven westwards across the sea. About midnight, the sailors sensed they

CHAPTER X

were approaching land. They took soundings finding the water one hundred and twenty feet deep. A short time later, they took soundings again. This time the water was ninety feet deep. Fearing they would be dashed against the rocks, they dropped four anchors from the stern and prayed for daylight.

In a panic, some of the crew pretended they were going to lower some anchors from the bow and attempted to escape from the ship, by letting the lifeboat down into the sea.

"Unless these men stay with the ship, you cannot be saved." Paul shouted to Julius and the soldiers.

A struggle broke out on the foredeck as the soldiers cut the ropes that held the lifeboat and let it drift away.

Just before dawn, Paul urged them all to eat.

"For the last fourteen days," he said, "you have been in constant suspense and have gone without proper food. You haven't eaten anything. Now I urge you to take some food. You need it to survive. Not one of you will lose a single hair from his head."

After he said this, he took some bread and gave thanks to God in front of them all. Then he broke it and began to eat. This encouraged them to eat some food themselves. When they had eaten as much as they could, someone suggested they lighten the ship by throwing the last of the cargo of grain into the sea.

Daylight came and they could see land, but no one recognised it.

"I can see a bay with a sandy beach," shouted a crew member pointing desperately at the horizon. "If we make towards it, we can run the ship aground there."

"Cut loose the anchors," commanded the captain, "and untie

THE STORY OF PAUL III

the ropes holding the rudders. Hoist the foresail to the wind and make for the beach."

There was a flurry of activity all over the decks as the exhausted crew tried to follow the captain's orders. Suddenly, they were all thrown violently to the deck as the ship struck a sandbar and ran aground. The bow stuck fast and would not move. The stern took the full force of the waves and started breaking into pieces by the pounding surf.

"We must kill all the prisoners in case they swim ashore and escape," said one of the soldiers to Julius.

"No! Release them all and allow them up on deck. Paul has said everyone will survive. We have to trust his God. He has been right about everything he has said thus far." Julius turned to Lysias and asked, "Do you agree, sir? You are the senior officer here."

Without hesitation, Lysias nodded and took command.

"Order those who can swim to jump overboard first and get to land," said Lysias. "The rest will have to get ashore the best they can, maybe on planks or on other pieces of the ship."

As the ship shuddered beneath their feet, groups of terrified men plunged into the water. Many screamed and cried out to their gods to save them. Others clung to the sides of the ship because they could not swim. It looked as if there would be a huge loss of life.[59]

Staggering to retail his footing Lysias said to Paul.

"I hope your god can do this. If not, and many die, I will personally make sure you join them if you make it to the beach alive."

CHAPTER XI

Paul lay exhausted in the waves on the edge of the beach. Aristarchus helped him onto his feet and pulled him out of the water. Lucas was already on land assisting a sailor who had nearly drowned in the surf. The beach was covered with flotsam and jetsam from the wreck and the bodies of sailors and prisoners alike.

Lucas started to check the men laying on the beach and was amazed none had drowned. They were exhausted and in shock, but they had not drowned. Julius sat with his head in his hands on the beach. Next to him lay Lysias retching, vomiting up sea water and groaning.

Groups of local people from the island started appearing and were walking down the beach checking the survivors. They gave them water and bread to eat. They also wrapped them in blankets and cloaks as a number were naked and shivering in the cold wind, which was still blowing. Having brought dry kindling and wood, the locals soon had several fires burning, and the survivors began to huddle together for warmth.

The locals were surprised such a large group of people had survived. The captain of the ship appeared and talked with Julius. Between them, they did a head count.

"How many dead or missing?" asked Lysias.

"None, sir. All two hundred and seventy-six are accounted for," said the captain. "I can't believe it. Not one person lost. Never in all my years at sea have I experienced something like this."

Lysias stood speechless looking from Paul to Lucas.

Julius looked at Paul, his eyes full of fear.

"Who are you? Which god is protecting you? Or are you a god?"

He and the captain dropped to their knees before Paul in awe and terror.

"Get up, men! I am no god," said Paul. "I serve the living God who is Father of all and his son Jesus called the Christ. He is the one we proclaim and the one you should worship. He is the one who has spared us today because he loves us. Now come on, you men, get up. You have your men to care for."

The wind had begun to drop, and the fires were burning out. So, Paul started gathering brushwood to put on the fire. Unknown to him, a snake was hiding in the bundle he had gathered. As he was about to throw the bundle on the fire, the snake, driven out by the heat, bit him and fastened itself to his hand. Paul quickly shook the snake off and it fell into the fire.

When the islanders saw the snake hanging from his hand, they were shocked and several loudly shouted.

"This man must be a murderer. He escaped drowning in the sea, but the goddess Justice has not allowed him to live and sent a snake to kill him."

The people expected him to swell or suddenly convulse and fall dead. When nothing unusual happened to him, they were astonished and changed their minds.

CHAPTER XI

"He must be a god," they whispered to one other, and fear swept through them.

The sailors and survivors from the wrecked ship gathered around amazed. Paul was not writhing in agony; he just stood there unconcerned. Some of them knelt in front of him in fear.

"I am not a god. I am a man just like you. Get up and listen to me," said Paul. With this, he began to tell them about Jesus.

The news of the wreck spread quickly in the nearby villages and the survivors were taken to people's homes in the area. Publius, the chief official of the island had an estate nearby and he came and invited the ship's owner, the captain, Julius and Lysias to his home. The centurion insisted he also include Paul, Lucas, and Aristarchus.

He welcomed them warmly to his home and showed them generous hospitality for three days.[60]

"I hear you are a physician, my father is sick in bed, suffering from fever and dysentery, I would value your help and advice." Publius explained.

Lucas asked Paul to join him, and they went to see the old man. Lucas examined him and turned to Paul.

"I think we need to pray for him; he is weak," said Lucas.

Paul placed his hands on the old man and prayed for his healing. Publius was anxiously watching his father. He noticed his breathing had changed and he seemed more at peace. Then his father opened his eyes and smiled at his son.

"Publius, my son, I would really like something to eat. I feel so much better," said the old man.

"This is astonishing," said Publius. "The fever has left him. Who are you that you can heal the sick?" he asked Paul.

∿∧∿∧∿

Winter had set in on the Island of Malta. Days of rain and wind kept most people in their own homes, but sickness tended to breed in those conditions. As news of the healing of Publius' father spread around the island, soon anyone who was sick started coming to the governor's house asking for help from Paul and his two friends. They prayed for everyone, and Lucas advised people how to avoid getting sick. Large numbers of people were healed and started following the teachings of Jesus. Publius was one of the first to embrace Paul's teaching.

Another who embraced Paul's message was the centurion, Julius. He had watched Paul and his two friends throughout the voyage and the shipwreck. He had seen things his head could not explain, and he observed the reaction of people on the island of Malta, most notably the island's governor, Publius. Towards the end of winter, Julius asked to be baptised and confessed he had become a follower of Jesus.

"I have something else I need to confess to you," he said to Paul after he had been baptised.

"What is it, Julius?" asked Paul.

"Well, we lost everything in the shipwreck, didn't we?" he said.

"Yes, I know," said Paul, who was beginning to wonder what was troubling him.

"I lost the satchel of letters I was taking to Rome, including the one written by Porcius Festus about you, the accusations against

CHAPTER XI

you and your appeal to Caesar."

Julius looked embarrassed and did not know how Paul would react.

"It means I don't know what to say or do with you when we get to Rome. There are no written charges, no explanation… Paul, there is no reason for you to appeal to Caesar."

∿∿∿

The captain of the ship and its owner had gone to the main town of the island and were trying to secure another vessel. The prisoners had all been moved to the security of a military barracks on the island and Julius had handed them over to the senior officer to have them sent to Rome in the spring.

Lysias, however, was another story. He steadily withdrew into himself. He stopped talking and avoided contact with everyone. He would only talk briefly with Lucas. He shunned every invitation from Publius to join them for meals. He seemed to be sinking deeper and deeper into some sort of despair. One day Lucas went to his room and encouraged him to come out into the spring sunshine and sit with him in Publius' garden.

Lucas cast a medical eye on him. His face was drawn and his cheeks hollow. He had not shaved for a few days and his chin was stubbly. He needed a bath as he smelt somewhat.

"Lysias, my friend, I don't know what is going on inside you, but you look awful on the outside," said Lucas. "And if you don't mind me saying, you smell awful."

For a brief moment, a smile crossed Lysias' face and he

looked at Lucas.

"Thank you for your encouraging words, doctor. They make me feel so much better," said Lysias sarcastically. "What do you prescribe for a malady of the heart?"

"Well, to start with, get up and come with me. We are going to the baths," said Lucas.

"No! No, I can't, all those people."

Lucas could hear real panic in Lysias' voice.

"Not the public baths, you ass. Publius' baths here at the house. You need to clean up, have a shave and you will feel better. No argument. Doctor's orders."

They went back into the villa, crossed the atrium, and headed to the wing containing the baths. On the way, Lucas called for two of the household slaves to attend them in the bath suite.

They went into the antechamber and undressed and began the bathing process. First, they went into the caldarium, which was heated by a brazier underneath the hollow floor. They sat next to each other on the bench and let the heat of the room do its work. Soon, they were sweating heavily and stepped out into the next room which contained cold-water basins where they could cool down.

Lysias was still not talking but grunted as Lucas chatted away. They returned to the caldarium for a bit longer before finally entering the cooler tepidarium, where the two household slaves awaited them. The two friends lay on raised tables where the slaves massaged them with scented oils.

The process was soothing and calming. Lysias began to relax somewhat.

CHAPTER XI

"Before we are done, you need a shave," said Lucas.

One of the slaves stepped forward with a large blade ready to shave Lysias' stubble.

In an instant, Lysias leapt to his feet and grabbed the blade out of the stunned slave's hand. He tried to attack the man with the knife. The slickness of his oiled body meant he lost his grip and skidded on the marble tiles, falling backwards onto the floor. He curled up into a foetal ball and started to sob uncontrollably.

Lucas sent the slaves out of the room and sat down on the floor beside the distraught man. Without saying anything to Lysias, he gently placed a hand on his shoulder and silently prayed.

The deep sobbing continued for some time before finally subsiding.

"Come on, stand up. Let's get you cleaned up and we can go outside," said Lucas. He called the slaves back.

"Get the strigils," Lucas said to them. "We need to scrape off the oil, dirt and sweat. It's a strigil, Lysias, not a knife. No one is going to hurt you, and the razor will trim your chin. Is that okay?"

"I'm so sorry. I don't know what came over me," Lysias said to the anxious looking slave. "Please continue your work; I am fine now."

Lucas and Lysias stood, arms outstretched allowing the slaves to scrape their naked, glistening bodies with the metal strigil removing the oil and sweat. Lysias sat as the man shaved his face. Finally, they both stood and walked to the large plunge pool of cold water and jumped in to conclude their bath.

A few minutes later, they were dressed and refreshed with Lysias looking much better. They sat under an awning in the garden and a servant brought them chilled wine and honey and cashew cakes.

THE STORY OF PAUL III

"Are you able to talk about what happened in there?" asked Lucas.

Lysias continued eating. After a long silence, he said.

"I feel so embarrassed crying like I did. It's such a sign of weakness. My father told me I was such a weakling when I cried."

"Tears fall for a reason," said Lucas. "They are our body's way of releasing toxins which build up in our heart. They are not a sign of weakness; tears are therapeutic and healing. I have seen this many times in people. Don't be afraid of your tears, Lysias."

"The thing is," Lysias continued. "I cry so much. I hide my tears and bury my emotions."

"That sounds like hard work to me," said Lucas. "Do you know why you cry?"

"I have no idea. My father always said I was weak and every time I cried, he mocked me and tried to toughen me up. He said I needed to grow up, get stronger and not give in to my weaknesses. He had a career planned for me. He wanted me to join the army. As you know, Philippi was full of Roman military veterans since the time of the civil war between Octavius and Mark Antony a hundred years ago. He wanted me to be like them. He wanted me to become a soldier, a Roman soldier.

"I didn't want to be a soldier," said Lysias. "I remember one day Father and I were bathing just like we were earlier. I told him I did not want to join the army. He became angry and we argued. I became emotional and began to cry. While I was crying, my dog heard me and wandered into the bath house. He put his chin on my knee and looked at me. I cried even more. My father became furious; he was beside himself with anger. He grabbed a shaving knife off the table and before I could do anything, he grabbed my

CHAPTER XI

dog and slit his throat and threw him on the floor in front of me. Then my father shouted,

"That will give you something to cry for. Now grow up and be a man, you great cry baby."

"The next day, I found my dog nailed to the door of the bath house."

Lysias' eyes filled with tears again.

"I have hated my father ever since. Whenever I see blood, my heart races. I feel sick and I think of my father. The hate comes back, and I can hardly control myself.

"I left home and joined the army as you know. My father said nothing. I progressed in Rome. I bought my citizenship and was appointed a military tribune. He knew, but he never congratulated me. I was sent to Jerusalem for my first posting. As soon as I arrived, I received news of his death back in Philippi. Not one tear fell from my eye. I thought, *Finally, I am free.* But of course, I am not free."

Lysias was silent for some time.

"What happened next?" asked Lucas.

"My first week in Jerusalem I had to oversee the crucifixion of a zealot. I had never done one before. It was horrific. Whoever thought up this method of execution was brutal. There was so much blood. It all comes back to me every time. My hatred of my father, my anger. I even have nightmares and see my dog nailed to a post.

"I have lost count of the number of crucifixions I have overseen. Then I met you and Paul and what do you talk to me about but your wretched crucified Galilean carpenter. And you ask me to believe in him!"

Lysias' voice rose as a mixture of anger, pain and sadness spilled out. He continued.

"Don't ask me to believe in this God you call father who had his son crucified to satisfy some ancient bloodlust," Lysias burst into tears again.

"I don't believe in the god you have described either,'" Lucas said gently. "The God I believe in and follow is a God of love, who passionately loves us and has done everything he can to bring us back home. He sent his only son, Jesus, the man from Nazareth, into our world to show us what God is really like. He is a Father unlike any human father. He does not mock us, taunt us, or make demands of us. He is love itself, the essence of love as we Greeks like to say."

Lucas paused before adding,

"You can come home, Lysias, if you let yourself be loved."

"So, you know all about me now, Lucas," said Lysias.

"Yes," replied Lucas. "And I love you too.

"It's easy to follow one who loves us so much. Love brings us home."

CHAPTER XII

The islanders honoured Paul in many ways. They collected money to help him on his way to Rome and introduced him to people all over the island. After three months, there was a small but thriving community of believers. Aristarchus had struck up a warm friendship with Publius and soon the two were regularly gathering people together and teaching them.

It became clear to Paul, Aristarchus would not be leaving Malta for quite some time. Julius secured another ship and they began preparations to leave the island.

"I'm sorry about the ship. It wintered here in the island," said Julius. "It is an Alexandrian ship with the figurehead of the twin gods Castor and Pollux that. But it won't be Castor and Pollux that get us safely to Rome, will it?" he laughed.

Not surprisingly, Aristarchus announced he was remaining behind to support Publius and the groups of believers in Jesus who were scattered across Malta.

Lysias told them he would accompany them to Rome, so he and Julius could ensure Paul got a fair hearing. When they were ready to sail, the islanders furnished them with the supplies they needed for the journey.

As had happened many times before when Paul boarded a ship, the believers escorted him to the vessel to bless him on his way.

The ship put out to sea and sailed to the island of Sicilia where they stopped at Syracuse and stayed for three days. From there, they set sail for the short crossing to Rhegium on the southern tip of the Italian mainland. The next day, a south wind came up, which took them swiftly along the coast and on the following day they entered a wide bay with islands scattered around.

"We are nearly home," said Julius. Standing on the deck with Lysias, Paul and Lucas, he pointed. "Look, do you see the mountain, the way it dominates the whole bay? We call it Vesuvius."

"Do you know this area, Julius?" asked Paul.

"Do I know it? I was born here. See the city on the southern flank of the mountain? I was born there. My parents live there… If they are still alive. I have not been home in a long time. It's coming into view now."

"What's the name of the city?" asked Lucas.

"Colonia Cornelia Veneria Pompeianorum, Pompeii for short. It is a beautiful place. Oh! This brings me such joy. We will sail to Puteoli, which is across the bay from the other city, Herculaneum, on the western flanks of the mountain."

Julius shared his extensive knowledge of the area, pointing out many of the coastal towns and islands around the bay.

"Do you see the island we are passing over there?" he asked. "It is Capri, where the Emperor Tiberius had his infamous Villa Jovis and carried on all sorts of scandalous activity. Look up there, you can see the villa. It's huge!

CHAPTER XII

"Straight ahead is Puteoli. For a long time, Puteoli was the largest transit port for Rome. It receives grain ships from Alexandria like this one. When I saw this ship in the harbour on Malta, I guessed it would be coming here. The city is in decline a bit since they started to develop Ostia and Portus further up the coast. But it will still be busy when we get there and the road to Rome will be full of wagons and transport."

"I heard there was a group of believers in Puteoli," said Paul. "I have relatives in Rome who know them."

"Who are your relatives?" asked Lucas.

"Their names are Andronicus and Junia. They are about my age, so they are getting on a bit," said Paul. "They were the ones who pioneered the spread of the good news in Rome and this area. They rank among the apostles as far as I am concerned. They were in Jerusalem on the day of Pentecost, all those years ago when the Holy Spirit was poured out and went back to Rome carrying the message. Andronicus and Junia were in Puteoli when Claudius expelled the Jews from Rome about ten years ago. When Priscilla and Aquila fled Rome for their safety, that is where they went before moving on to Corinth."

"Oh, that is how you know them," said Lucas. "Perhaps we can find some believers in Puteoli before we head on to Rome."

"I have an idea," said Julius. "If you can find some believers here then why not stay with them for a while. Since we're so close, I would like to take the opportunity to go to Pompeii to visit my family. It has been a long time. If you'd like, Paul, you're welcome to come and visit Pompeii with me."

"What does your family do in Pompeii?" asked Lucas.

"They have a beautiful house in the city as well as a number of farms inland," said Julius. "They are merchant traders selling their farm produce in the city, and they also run a bakery."

"Well, let us see what happens when we get to Puteoli," said Paul.

They gazed towards the land taking in the beauty of the bay and the tall mountain.

"Look! The harbour is in sight; we will dock soon," said Julius.

The ship slowly approached the harbour. The port was full of all sorts of shipping. This was the first flush of early spring boats to have risked the late winter crossing from Egypt and North Africa. The captain spotted a berth and soon the vessel was moored. An army of slaves descended on the boat under orders to unload the grain as quickly as possible.

The four passengers disembarked and pushed their way through the crowded port area into a large spacious market and forum.

"How will you find any of your followers of Jesus here?" asked Lysias.

"I would think we could see if there is a Jewish synagogue in the city as a first step," said Paul. "They may know of my relatives, but also they are duty bound to offer me hospitality as a fellow Jew. You three will not be welcomed because you are Gentiles."

"Well, that is no surprise to me," said Lysias. "Don't forget I was in charge in Jerusalem and Tiberius for quite a while, so I know how this works. But I can't pull rank here."

"Come on, Lysias," said Lucas, "leave it to Paul. He is used to this. Julius, do you know this place or anyone here? Can you make enquiries?"

CHAPTER XII

"Leave it to me, my friends. I'll see what I can find out. There is a tavern over there. Go get yourselves something to drink. I recommend the local wine; it's excellent. Order me a drink too and don't drink mine, I'll come back shortly."

The three men sat and ordered drinks. They also ordered olives, almonds, and some meatballs of indeterminate origin. When they arrived, Paul sniffed them warily.

"Don't worry," said Lucas taking a cautious bite, "the wine should help."

He chewed for a few moments, then said,

"Oh, my goodness! They are delicious. It's pork, I think. Err, sorry, Paul."

"No problem," said Paul, "I am free, and as this is nearly Rome, when in Rome, I will do as the Romans do."

Lysias laughed with his mouth full.

"I've never heard anyone say that before. It's a good one, but I doubt it will catch on."

The food and wine had all gone and Lysias was dozing at the table with his head on his arms when Julius returned.

"Here's Julius," said Lucas nudging Lysias awake. "What do you know?"

"Well, I went through the market to the forum over there," Julius pointed in the general direction of impressive buildings flanking the forum and agora. "There are numerous offices and banks in the lower rooms of the basilica. I went to the first one I saw and asked if there was a Jewish synagogue in the city."

THE STORY OF PAUL III

"And is there?" asked Paul excitedly.

"There is. It is no more than three insulae away, so I walked straight there," said Julius.

"Come, let us go there immediately," said Paul.

"No need," said Julius, "I have been there already. It is down a side alley off the main road through the city. I went and knocked on the door. A man answered, clearly a Jew, and I asked him outright if he knew if there were followers of Jesus the Nazarene in the city."

"How did he react?" asked Paul.

"Well, he became quite agitated and wanted to know why I wanted to know. At this point, a younger man appeared behind him and demanded what was going on. The older man started talking in Aramaic to the younger man. They had no idea I learnt some Aramaic in Judea and could follow their conversation."

Lysias laughed.

"I could never master the barbaric tongue. What did they say?"

"They were worried about me. The older man said to the younger not to tell me anything in case they got into trouble. Then they basically threw me out. So, I left and started to walk back here. No sooner than when I turned within five steps of the main street, the younger man ran around the corner and virtually bumped into me. He pulled me towards the wall and whispered in my ear. He said he knew where they could be found."

"Excellent news," said Paul. "How do we find them?"

"I don't know yet," said Julius. "The young man said he needed to finish something, then he would come and help us. He is joining us here in an hour or so. In the meantime, where is my drink?"

CHAPTER XII

In high spirits, the four friends ordered more food for Julius and more wine. True to his word, about an hour later, a young man appeared outside the tavern looking for Julius. Julius waved and beckoned him to the table. He stood in front of them looking from one to the other. Then he said,

"I have information for you, but it will cost you."

Lysias immediately stood looking angry, but Paul grabbed his arm.

"Sit down," Paul said, "let's hear what he has to say." Then turning to the fellow, Paul asked, "Are you a follower of Jesus?"

"No, I am not, but I know some who are. I can show you how to find them if you are willing to pay me."

Lucas took two coins out of his money bag and put them on the table.

Indignant, the young man said, "It will take more than that."

Lysias shifted in his seat and flicked back his cloak revealing a knife.

The young man grabbed the coins. "Err... No, this is fine."

"You need to follow the crosses," said the fellow.

"What do you mean?" asked Julius.

"Back at the junction of the road where the synagogue is, you will see a cross scratched into the curb stone. One of its arms will be longer. Go in the direction it points and keep following until you see the next. It will lead you to a house or shop where you can find these "Christians" as they are called around here." With that, he jumped up and ran out of the tavern.

"That is the strangest thing I have ever heard," said Paul.

"Come on, let's go. This could be fun," said Lysias.

Within half an hour they were standing outside a domus with a gate opening onto the street. On the pavement, in front of them, was the sixth cross they had found, and its long arm pointed directly at the house. They banged on the door and, shortly, a porter cautiously looked out the iron barred window in the doorway.

"What do you want?" he asked.

"We have followed the mark of the cross on the pavement and it has led us here," said Paul.

"What is your name?" he asked.

"Paul, Paul of Tarsus."

"Wait here," replied the porter.

In less than a minute, excited voices could be heard from inside and the door was suddenly thrown open.

"Paul! Paul, is it really you?" said an excited elderly lady.

"Junia! Yes, it's me. My dear cousin, how happy I am to see you," said Paul.

"Come in, come in, and your friends, you are welcome to our house. I am Junia, the widow of Andronicus."

It was the happiest of reunions for Paul and Junia as there was so much news to share. Many years had passed since they last met. Paul was saddened to learn of Andronicus' passing two years earlier.

"I moved down here to be part of the community of believers in this city after Andronicus died," Junia explained. "We left the believers in Rome in the capable hands of Priscilla and Aquila. There are many gatherings across the city. We were so excited to receive

CHAPTER XII

the wonderful letter you wrote to us several years ago. It brought so much clarity and revelation to us."

"I am going to Rome now," said Paul. "I have appealed to Caesar for him to hear my case. I am technically in custody of these two men. The Centurion Julius here, he is my gaoler. And Lysias, he is my accuser."

Both men grinned and then laughed.

In unison, they said, "No, I am not."

Julius explained the rather long and complicated story to Junia.

"We must send word to Rome to tell our friends you are here," said Junia. "It is at least a three-day journey unless we can secure a wagon or horse. When they hear you are coming, I am sure they will want to come and meet you to help you on the way. Now food, are you hungry?"

Lysias rubbed Paul's stomach. "Paul is always hungry."

Everyone laughed and soon they were reclining on couches as household servants brought dishes of food and more local wine.

"This wine is delicious," announced Lysias.

"It tastes like it is from the vineyards on the flanks of the mountain," said Julius.

"Indeed, it is," said Junia. "How do you know this?"

"I am from here. My family lives in Pompeii on the other side of Vesuvius."

"Oh!" said Junia. "What is your family name?"

"My father is Marcus Lucretius, a merchant in the city."

"Interesting," Junia's eyes twinkled. "Do you know a man named Meges?"

"Of course, I do. He is my father's freedman. He manages much of my father's business. How do you know him?" asked Julius.

"We have met a few times. Are you planning to visit your family?" she asked.

"Yes, I hope to go tomorrow, if Paul promises he won't run away and will still be here when I get back," Julius laughed.

"Do you mind if I come with you?" asked Lysias. "I would enjoy the journey."

The next morning Julius and Lysias acquired the use of two horses and were at Junia's gate.

As they mounted, Junia handed a sealed letter to Julius.

"Will you give this to Meges for me, young man?"

"Of course," said Julius.

"I presume you know the way, but just in case you get lost, just follow the crosses," she said smiling. Then she turned on her heel and went back inside as the porter closed the gate. Julius looked momentarily confused, then he suddenly guessed. Meges was a believer also.

Paul and Lucas spent almost a week with the believers in Puteoli. Word had been sent to Rome and a reply informed them some of the Christians in the city would meet them at the Forum of Appius, a two day walk from Rome. Paul taught and shared with the large group who gathered in Junia's home and the time passed quickly.

After six days, Julius and Lysias returned from Pompeii. Julius

CHAPTER XII

was eager to share his experience with Paul, Lucas and Junia.

"I suspect you know what happened," Julius said to Junia, who smiled warmly at him.

"After stopping to pay my respects at my family tombs just outside the city, we entered the city at the Porta Saliniensis on the road from Herculaneum. We dismounted and led the horses by their bridles."

"I spotted it first," said Lysias proudly. "A small cross carved into the stone right by the gate. After what you said, we naturally followed the cross and after a few minutes, it led us to a bakery."

"Not just any bakery," said Julius. "It was our family bakery! There was a cross on the pavement pointing at our bakery. I went in and asked for the tenant who rents it. He is new and I didn't know him. As we talked, I spotted a plaster mounting at the back of the counter on the wall. I asked the man about it, and he said something about it protecting the house and became vague."

"We left," interrupted Lysias. "The bakery is a corner shop with entrances to the south and west. Half the shops in the street seemed to have crosses on the pavements outside pointing in. I'm getting good at spotting these things. Then I saw another one pointing along the street into the centre of the city."

"It was the way we needed to go because it leads to my family home. We arrived at the street entrance to our house, and I was about to go in when Lysias saw it, on the pavement right in front of my house, a cross pointing directly into the entryway of our domus. The house of Marcus Lucretius, no less![61]

"It was wonderful to see my mother and father again, and my sister. We talked for hours but there was no mention of Jesus. In fact, my father still had the family altar in the peristyle lararium with statues to Jupiter, Hercules, Isis, and Neptune.

"I gave your letter to Meges," Julius said to Junia. "He was delighted to welcome me back home. He told me my parents knew of his faith and were sympathetic, but they adhere to the old gods. He also told me there were a number of believers in Pompeii. They call themselves Christians. The baker who was vague with me is one of their leaders!"[62]

Julius paused, reflecting. Then he said,

"You and your husband made a big impression on him."

Junia smiled again and nodded.

"Did you tell your parents about your new faith?" asked Paul.

"Did he ever," said Lysias. "He is really good at it. By the time he finished, I was ready to jump straight into the atrium pool to be baptised."

Paul looked surprised. Julius and Lysias grinned.

"He is just teasing you, Paul," said Julius. "But he is not far off. Are you, Lysias? As for my parents, my mother and sister were open, but my father was distant and annoyed. He is a man of influence in the city and is aware of his position. I hope to return there one day after we have finished our business with you in Rome, Paul."

After a few moments of silence Julius looked again at Paul.

"When do we depart for the capital?"

CHAPTER XIII

Early the next morning Paul and his travelling companions departed for Rome. They decided to walk as the weather was improving and the number of grain carts and wagons on the road heading north to Rome often became ensnarled in backups and delays. Walking enabled them to bypass the worst of the congestion. Soon the road joined the Via Appia, the oldest of the roads originating in the centre of Rome in the Forum Romanum. They continued northwards as the road swung towards the coast at Tarracina at the sixty-sixth milestone south of Rome. Alongside the road ran a canal which went as far as the Forum of Appius.

"Thank goodness we have reached the canal," said Julius. "We can use one of the canal boats that pass through the Pontine Marshes. The marshes are infested with mosquitos. The least amount of time we can spend in there, the better. The canal boats continue through the night drawn by mules so we will be at the Forum by tomorrow."

Not long after dawn the canal boat arrived at the Forum. With the muleteers making so much noise through the night, no one in Paul's party had much sleep. As soon as they disembarked, they began looking for familiar faces. Lucas led the way.

"Let's go to the market in the centre and see if we recognise anyone."

The group entered a large, busy, and crowded market, full of noise and people. Within a few minutes, people they knew were waving and pushing their way towards them.

"Paul! Paul! Luke!" shouted a familiar voice. "Over here!"

"Aquila, Priscilla, thank God you are here. I am so glad to see you," said Paul.

Other friends of Paul and Lucas had accompanied Aquila and Priscilla. Apelles, the young man sent by Paul to Rome from Corinth, Epenetus from Ephesus, Ampliatus, and Urbanus, and Paul's dear friend, Stachys.

"How good to see you all," Paul exclaimed.

After warm embraces and introductions were made to Lysias and Julius, they journeyed north another ten miles. Everyone chattered nonstop until the party reached the Three Taverns at the thirty-third mile post where the slightly less energetic were waiting. Tryphena, Tryphosa, Persis, Philologus, and Julia were a few of those waiting at the tavern. More greetings and more embracing ensued.[63]

Forming one large happy band of brothers and sisters, they continued to Rome. Julius and Lysias took up the rear of the group. As they neared Rome, the two of them spoke in low voices about what they should do with Paul once they reached the city.

The nearer they got to the city, the busier the Via Appia became.

"We need to talk with Paul before we get into the city," said Julius. "Let's run ahead and catch up with him and Lucas and the fellow Aquila and his wife. They seem to be the leaders of this group. We need to have a plan."

Julius and Lysias quickly caught up with the group when they

CHAPTER XIII

sat in the shade of a cypress tree to eat and drink.

"Before we enter the city, we need to decide how we handle your appeal to Caesar," said Julius. "As you know, I am the one charged with bringing you before the authorities, but I have lost the letter sent by Festus in the shipwreck."

"And I am the one who arrested you in Jerusalem and sent you, two years earlier, to Felix," said Lysias. "Technically, I am the one who has the evidence of your so-called crimes."

"What we don't know," said Paul, "is if the leaders of the Sanhedrin in Jerusalem have sent any word to the Jews in Rome about my case."

"Lysias and I have a plan we would like to propose," said Julius. "We suggest immediately upon entering Rome you go to a safe house somewhere. Perhaps you know a place, Aquila?"

"We know just the place," said Aquila, Priscilla nodded her agreement.

"I need to know where it is as I will need to be your guard. While your case is being dealt with, the law requires you be under guard. Can you make enquiries among the Jewish community to discover if any news or official contact has come from Jerusalem?" asked Julius.

"The problem with the Jews in Rome," answered Aquila, "is there is no single body ruling over the whole Jewish community in the city. There are leaders of different synagogues, and we know several of them, though they are suspicious of us as we are what they call followers of the sect of the Nazarene."

"When we get settled, maybe as a visiting rabbi, I could send messages to them and ask them to visit me," said Paul.

"Julius and I will go to the Palatine and find the office dealing with Imperial audiences and make enquiries," said Lysias. "Don't worry, Paul. I am sure it will not be a problem."

"I am not worried. I know Caesar himself needs to hear the message of Jesus," said Paul.

"It might not be quite as easy as you think with this emperor," said Julius.

They set off again and soon the high city walls appeared before them. They passed through the Servian Walls by way of the Porta Capena and within a few moments they were standing at the southern end of the vast arena of the Circus Maximus.

"This is my first visit to Rome; I am so excited to be here." Lucas pointed to their right. "What is that large building up there?"

"It's the Imperial Palace of our illustrious emperor Nero Claudius Caesar Augustus Germanicus, the fifth Roman emperor since the fall of the republic," said Lysias. His voice was heavy with sarcasm.

"Careful now, my friend," said Julius. "Rome has ears everywhere and any hint of irony or sarcasm like that can land you in trouble."

"Me, sarcastic? Never!" grinned Lysias.

"We go this way," said Aquila pointing in the opposite direction. "We have friends and a place for you to stay on Mons Aventine. It's safe and there is a wonderful view across the Circus Maximus towards the Palatine and the palaces opposite. On a race day you might even get to see the chariot races."

The group of Roman Christians who had travelled with Paul from the forum of Appius dispersed and went their separate ways. Paul and his three friends accompanied Aquila and his wife to the

CHAPTER XIII

suburb on Aventine Hill.

They climbed up through the narrow streets of the Aventine past tenements five or six floors high. Paul had never seen such high dwellings. The streets were crowded and noisy. The ground floors were nearly all workshops and food shops typical of every Roman city Paul had visited. Soon they turned into a side alley where the buildings remained crammed together but were owned by wealthier people. They arrived at the street entry of a large domus and banged on the door. The security window opened, and a face looked out. After recognising the faces of Aquila and Priscilla, the porter swung open the door.

"Is your master at home?" asked Aquila.

"Yes, he has been expecting you for some days. All is prepared," said the porter. "Come inside and wait here. I will go and call him."

The porter returned accompanied by an elderly man and woman.

"Welcome, Paul," said the old man.

"Nereus! It's been so long," said Paul. "And this must be your sister?"

"Yes, indeed. This is my sister Lucina," said Nereus.

"As Lucina, the widow of Macrinus, I too welcome you, Paul. I do not usually live here with my brother. I live on my estate beyond the second mile post outside the city on the Via Ostiensis, which is much quieter than this place. We wonder if you might like to stay there rather than in the busy city."

"Thank you, Lady," said Julius. "It might be good but until we can settle the matter of Paul's appeal to the Emperor, it is best he stays in the city. May I lodge here also as his official guard?"

"Of course. There is room for these other two men also. Who, may we ask, are you?" asked Nereus.

"My apologies," said Paul. "This is my dear friend Lucas from Philippi, my traveling companion and my good doctor."

Lucas bowed.

"And this is my dear friend Tribune Claudius Lysias, lately from the Province of Judea."

"I am honoured, sirs, to have you in my home," said Nereus. "You are most welcome. Come, let us go through to the peristyle where we can take refreshment."

They walked along a corridor with a beautifully paved mosaic floor which opened into a classic atrium. A fountain in the centre of the rainwater pool danced and added movement to the water. Nereus led the way further through the house into a garden walled on three sides by a colonnaded peristyle. The fourth side was open and had a breath-taking view across the city of Rome.

They all stood in awe of the view before them. In front, at the bottom of the hill was the whole expanse of the Circus Maximus. To their left, they could see the river Tiber weaving its way through the city with huge bridges spanning it. They could see the Capitoline Hill with the enormous temple dedicated to Jupiter gleaming white as the sun reflected on the dazzling marble. It was over six hundred years old.

A vast array of buildings sprawled across the Palatine Hill which were the Imperial Palaces dating back to the time of Julius Caesar and Augustus. To their right, on another hill, stood the unfinished Temple of Claudius which Nero was remodelling as a massive water feature.

CHAPTER XIII

Paul stared in wonder at this sight.

He turned to Lucas,

"At last, I have come to Rome. And here I can also preach the good news of Jesus, even to the emperor himself. God willing."

Tears welled in Paul's eyes.

"How I have longed for this day

∿∿∿

Over the next three days, messages were sent to small home groups of believers across the city to find out about the various Jewish leaders known to Aquila and Priscilla. Paul needed to know if they would be antagonistic towards him.

"We cannot invite them to this house if they are just as hostile as the Jerusalem assassins," Paul said. "I have chosen to explain my situation to a small group of these Jewish leaders on my own terms. I don't want to have another riot, which might complicate my formal appeal."

Three days later, a small group of local Jewish leaders arrived at the house on the Aventine. Julius had decided he needed to sit in on the discussion in his role as Paul's guard.

"This might sound excessive but to demonstrate your position as plaintiff, I think a small chain on your wrist might add some drama," said Lysias.

After the leaders assembled, Paul addressed them and explained why he had come to Rome.

"My brothers, although I have done nothing against our people or against the customs of our ancestors, I was arrested in Jerusalem and handed over to the Romans." Paul nodded in the direction of Julius who tried his best to look stern and official.

"The authorities examined me and wanted to release me because I was not guilty of any crime deserving death. However, the Jewish leaders in Jerusalem objected, so I was compelled to make an appeal to Caesar. I certainly did not intend to bring any charge against my own people."

They listened intently as he spoke and occasionally glanced at one another.

"I have asked to see you and talk with you for this reason," Paul lifted his arm and continued. "It is because of the hope of Israel that I am bound with this chain."

"We have not received any letters from Judea concerning you," said one of them.

"None of our people who have come from there has reported or said anything bad about you," said another. "But we want to hear what your views are, for we know people everywhere are talking against this sect of the Nazarene."

After the Jewish leaders left, Paul, Julius and Lysias walked back into the garden and sat in the shade of the peristyle discussing the plan further.

"It is good to hear nothing untoward has come from Jerusalem," said Lysias. "It has been over two and a half years. Perhaps this has gone quiet because you have been out of sight for so long, Paul."

"My main concern is Festus," said Julius. "He may have sent a letter overland to Rome to alert them of your arrival," said Julius.

CHAPTER XIII

"We left Caesarea almost five months ago and it has been winter. Letters from the eastern provinces at worst can take up to three months this time of the year."

Lysias chimed in. "I suggest you and I go the Palatine, Julius. We need to find the office dealing with appeals to Caesar. There must be hundreds of people with a lawsuit or conflict, and everyone wants the emperor to hear their case personally. I am sure there is large department dealing with this sort of thing.

"If Nero is like every other emperor, he will only deal personally with the cases he thinks can make him money or those with land or an estate to confiscate to fatten his own coffers. He won't be interested in an unknown Jewish rabbi from Judaea, to be honest. I'm sorry, Paul, but you just aren't that important, even if you are a Roman citizen."

"I understand what you are saying," said Paul. "When you are far away in Judaea, the grand gesture of appealing to the emperor sounds impressive. But when I sit here and look across this huge city and see the size of the Imperial Palace over there on the hill, I realise, this must all seem rather small."

"Yes, you are probably right," said Julius. "But we want to resolve it so you can be free to go wherever the Father leads you. I have not known you long and I am only beginning to know God as my Father. This is all new to me, but I believe he has brought us together for a reason. I think we are meant to help you at this time of your life, Paul. Even you, Lysias."

"Is that so?" Lysias chuckled, "Even a reprobate like me!"

"I don't recall anyone calling you a reprobate," said Paul.

"That's because you don't know me," added Lysias.

"I know you enough to know you are not a reprobate. You have a warm and tender heart which has been deeply wounded," said Paul.

Lysias looked away at the view across the city. When he looked back at Paul, there were tears in his eyes.

"Has Lucas been talking about me?" he said.

"No, he doesn't need to," Paul replied. "It's written all over you."

"Well, anyway, Julius and I have a job to do," said Lysias. "We can't spend all day sitting here talking. Come on, Julius. We're off to see the Emperor, or someone."

Lysias stood, grabbed Julius by the arm and marched him back into the house.

∿∿∿

Within a few minutes, the two men were striding down the hill into the valley below. They took the street flanking the Circus Maximus close to the river and through the market and Forum Boarium with its ancient circular temple of Hercules Victor.

"I wonder what will become of all these temples to the various gods if Paul's teaching about his risen Galilean carpenter every really takes hold here," mused Lysias as they made their way through the streets.

They turned right into the main road leading into the Forum Romanum and walked past the Temple of Castor and Pollux. They came out into the crowded teeming heart of Rome.

"Come on. This way, Lysias, through the arch of Augustus and up the hill," said Julius. "The office we need is up there on the Palatine Hill, follow me up these steps."

CHAPTER XIII

Soon they were standing in a crowded courtyard in front of an imposing building. Praetorian guards stood on either side of the entryway and appeared to be stopping most people from entering the building. They walked forward. Both were dressed in military clothes they acquired soon after arriving in Rome.

"Halt!" said one of the guards. "Where do you think you are going? Who are you?"

"I am the Military Tribune Claudius Lysias from the Province of Judea, and I am here along with this Centurion of the Italian Regiment sent by his excellency Porcius Festus, Procurator and Governor of Judea."

"Never heard of him," sniggered the other guard.

"We are here to petition the emperor concerning a case from Judaea," added Julius.

"Everyone here is petitioning the emperor about something, join the line," said the guard. Then, he pushed them aside.

"But tell me, who handles these petitions?" asked Lysias.

When the guard realised Lysias would not be fobbed off, he relented.

"Wait a minute, seeing as how you are military, I'll tell you this," said the Praetorian. "These crowds are all civil cases. Military is handled somewhere else. Yours sounds military to me. My advice is to go down the corridor over there where there is an office that might help you. Come on. Go through there, just don't tell them I let you through. I don't want any trouble."

Within a few steps, Lysias and Julius were out of the bustle of the crowded courtyard walking through one of the lower subterranean corridors of the vast Imperial Palace. Whenever they came to a door, a guard stopped them, and they asked for the military petitions' office. Finally, they came to a door, and they were informed they were in the right place. They knocked on the door before placing their ears against it. A voice from inside shouted, "Enter." They entered a bright room lit by a shaft of light from high above in the ceiling.

"What do you want," asked a voice with a Greek accent.

By his demeanour and clothing, the man looked like a Greek Imperial freedman, one of the hundreds of minor officials who staffed the complex administrative bureaucracy at the heart of the Empire.

Lysias explained as best he could.

"Well, you are in the right place," said the man.

"I am Crassus, one of the emperor's freedman. I am also a magistrate empowered by the Emperor to resolve issues like this. I decide if it goes higher up or not. My word is final. Is that clear?"

Julius and Lysias offered a curt nod.

"The Procurator was Porcius Festus, you say."

Crassus went over to a rack of shelves stuffed with scrolls. Mumbling and cursing, he rummaged through them.

"Nothing on file from a Festus in Judaea. Are you sure you got his name right?

Julius nodded and told him of Festus' recent appointment and explained again Paul's situation.

"So, let me get this right. Your man has appealed to the emperor,"

CHAPTER XIII

continued the bureaucrat. "He is a citizen. A Jew. You arrested him."

He pointed at Lysias.

"You say the Jews in Jerusalem accused him of some crime or other. You say he had committed no obvious crime, but to avoid being assassinated by these Jews you sent him off to Caesarea Maritima. Thinking he would save his skin, he appealed to Caesar as is his right of course. Am I right so far?"

Lysias and Julius both nodded.

"You were given the task of escorting him to Rome, am I right?" he said pointing at Julius.

Julius nodded.

"You say the governor sent a letter about this case? Give me the letter."

"I am sorry, sir. I don't have it. We were shipwrecked and it got lost," Julius explained.

The man sat down heavily in a chair.

"Oh, for the love of Jupiter. Let me get this right."

Pointing at Lysias, he said.

"You arrested him even though you say he was innocent."

Pointing at Julius, he said,

"You brought him here and have lost the letter, and you say the Jews in Rome have never heard of him."

He paused and looked intently at them both. Then said,

"It amazes me Rome has conquered the whole world with people like you two in its army. Do you think the emperor would give a moment's thought to a case like this? Our illustrious emperor has far more important things to do such as enter his latest poem in some ridiculous poetry competition or compete in the next chariot races in the Circus Maximus."

He wrote something on a sheet of papyrus and handed it to them.

"Appeal to the emperor denied, no charges to answer. Now get out of my sight, both of you. And stop wasting people's time. Next!" he shouted as they left the room.

A line had already formed outside the door and another group went in.

They climbed back up the Aventine Hill to the house of Nereus. A group had gathered to await their arrival. Anxious eyes all turned towards them as they entered.

"Paul," said Lysias, "you are a free man. Your appeal was denied. You are free to live and do as you please. Somehow, I think your Galilean Carpenter is quite pleased."

"But I wanted to preach to the emperor," said Paul.

"I think that will have to wait for another time," said Lysias. "Nereus, have you got any decent wine in the house? I'm parched. I'm dying for a drink. I think this calls for a celebration."

CHAPTER XIV

Over the next few days, Paul struggled to adjust to his new reality. He sat with Lucas one day in Nereus' garden overlooking the city. He was in a dark mood.

"More than three years has passed since we left Corinth for Jerusalem," he said to Lucas. "We made brief visits on the way east to Macedonia and Troas. We bypassed Ephesus and met the leaders on the beach at Miletus. I remember weeping with them and thinking I would never see them again. We had collected so much money for the poor in Jerusalem. It took a whole gang of us to transport it to them. When we gave it to the elders, do you remember how they reacted, Lucas?"

"Yes, I do," said Lucas. "They hardly said thank you. They were more interested in trying to show you were a law-abiding Jew rather than a law breaker."

"Exactly, I did as they suggested and ended up being arrested, and then languished under guard in Caesarea Maritima for the best part of two years. Do you know the leaders in Jerusalem never came to visit me once the whole time I was there? It's like they shunned me."

"I don't think they shunned you, Paul," said Lucas. "I think James, in particular, didn't know what to do. I think he was embarrassed by the whole incident in the Temple. I met him, remember? He took me to Galilee to meet his mother, Mary. In many ways, he is a gifted and kind man, but he has remained entrenched in his Jewish background and upbringing."

"There it is, you see," added Paul. "James may be the brother of our Lord, but he is under the influence of those Pharisees who claim to be believers. You and I know how they have dogged my every turn trying to undermine my teaching and pervert the truth of the gospel. They don't want freedom; they want tradition and law. They have been false brothers all along. If I give in to them, the gospel will become nothing but a sect within Judaism. I have heard them call it the Nazarene sect."

Paul's mood became darker as he reflected and brooded over the last few years. He sighed heavily.

"I'm sorry, Lucas. It's all a bit painful today. Some days, I sense the Spirit's presence, I hear his voice of comfort and know he is with me, then there are days like today when it is all so bleak."

"Can I pray for you, Paul," asked Lucas.

Paul grunted, which Lucas took to be an affirmative.

"Father, I ask you to come right now to your dear son Paul and hold him in your arms. Father, will you pour your love into his heart and meet him in his pain and disappointment. Thank you that in his weakness you really are his strength."

As Lucas prayed, tears began to run down Paul's cheeks.

"My grand appeal to Caesar, which seemed such a master stroke at the time, has come to nothing," Paul said between his sobs. "Now what am I to do? I have looked forward to coming here for so long. I wrote to them from Corinth those years ago. There are so many

CHAPTER XIV

groups of believers across this city. Aquila and Priscilla and the others have done such a wonderful work. The reality is, they don't need me. There is nothing left for me to do here."

After a while, Paul's mood seemed to lift a little. A servant brought them a bowl of fruit and he and Lucas cracked open a juicy pomegranate. Its sweetness filled his mouth. Nereus and his sister Lucina entered the garden and were chatting together as she picked roses and placed them in a basket. They came over to where Paul and Lucas were sitting.

"May we join you?" Nereus asked.

"Please do," said Paul.

"I have news," said Nereus. "I have received word from some of those leaders who came to meet you last week. They would like to come back and hear more from you. Would you be open to this?"

Lucas grinned and nudged Paul.

"Nothing to do, Paul? Let's see what Father has in mind."

Word got around that Paul was willing to meet with the Jewish leaders and they arranged a day to come. To everyone's amazement, a large number turned up to Nereus' house. Paul welcomed them and began explaining about the kingdom of God. He started from the Law of Moses and went on to the Prophets to show them how everything pointed to Jesus. Paul started talking to them in the morning and continued on into the evening. Nereus' servants kept them supplied with food and drink all through the day.

At times during the day, especially as they shared a meal together, it became obvious that some of their hearts were opening to the Spirit and were convinced by what Paul was saying. But not all.

During the questions and discussions over the meal, disagreements emerged among themselves. Paul was frustrated by the way some of them so quickly retreated into their minds rather than their hearts. As the sun set, he made a final statement,

"The Holy Spirit spoke the truth to your ancestors when he said through Isaiah the prophet,

'Go to this people and say,

You will be ever hearing but never understanding;

you will be ever seeing but never perceiving.

For this people's heart has become calloused;

they hardly hear with their ears, and they have closed their eyes.

Otherwise, they might see with their eyes, hear with their ears,

understand with their hearts and turn, and I would heal them.'

"Therefore, I want you to know that God's salvation has been sent to the Gentiles, and they will listen."

Paul's frustration spilled out in this last statement. Some took offence and stood up to leave, ritually shacking their prayer shawls as a sign of rejection and disapproval. Others stayed and came back many more times. They invited Paul to teach in their synagogues and into their homes. Paul had found his ministry again.[64]

It continued like this for several weeks. Paul felt he might have outstayed his welcome at Nereus' home. But Nereus assured him this was not the case. One day Paul said to Lucas.

"When I first went to Corinth, I worked with Aquila in his tentmaking business. It gave me something to do when I was not teaching and it provided me a chance to earn money and pay for

CHAPTER XIV

my keep. It also meant I could save some money to help fund my journeys. I have never wanted to be a burden to anyone."

"No one considers you a burden, Paul." Lucas reassured him. "But I also understand your need for funds. We know we don't do this for the money, but we can't do it without the money. I have been practicing as a physician since coming to Rome and I get paid for what I do."

"I am thinking I might talk with Aquila and Priscilla and see if I can work with them as before. Then maybe I could rent a house somewhere in the city for myself," Paul said. "I think if I could do this long enough, I could save money to maybe return to the east or even go on to Spain. It has always been in my heart to go there."

∿∿∿

One afternoon, Julius came to see Paul.

"I have decided to resign my position as a centurion," he said. "I enjoyed the army before, but ever since I met you, Paul, and came to know Jesus, I have wanted to share this with my family and friends. After I went to see them in Pompeii, on our way here, I knew I wanted to go back there. In my father's household, his chief steward Meges is a follower of Jesus. I am feeling my heavenly Father wants me to go home to my natural father. What do you think?"

"You would go with my blessing," said Paul. "I will miss you, my beloved guard."

Not long after Julius' departure, Lucas came to see Paul. He too was wanting to move on.

"I want to go back to Philippi for a while," said Lucas.

"I am not surprised, Lucas. I have felt your restlessness. I do not see your future as a Roman doctor. I have been thinking too about the other work you have been writing, the one you left behind with Theophilus in Caesarea. Maybe you should finish it."

"My thoughts exactly, Paul," he answered. "When I began it, I wrote what Jesus said to his followers just as he was about to ascend back to his Father. He said, 'and you will be my witnesses in Jerusalem, and in all Judea and Samaria, and to the ends of the earth.' This has formed the structure of the work. It begins in Jerusalem and Judea, then Samaria, Philip's story, Cornelius' story and of course, your story and your travels taking the message across the world."

"Now here we are at the ends of the earth, in many ways," said Paul.

"I never intended to write down the stories of all the apostles, or your whole story, to be honest. But I do want to write about our journey to Rome and of course, I need to go back to Theophilus' place to do it. To me, it seems like a good place to conclude the work."

"When do you plan to leave?" asked Paul.

"Soon, before the winter comes. I don't want to travel to the east during winter if I can avoid it. What about you, Paul? What are your plans?"

"I've been here almost six months and you can see how the door has opened to me. I will stay for at least two years, I think. I have my own rented house. I am able to teach and proclaim God's kingdom boldly and without hindrance," said Paul.

"I like the way you say this. I think I have an idea how to end my second volume," exclaimed Lucas.

CHAPTER XIV

"There is something else, Paul," said Lucas. "Lysias and I have been talking too. He is so close to becoming a follower of Jesus. In reality, I think he already is, but he won't admit it. I feel he has unfinished business in Philippi. He has not been back since his father died. He needs to lay something to rest there."

"Of course, we know some of his family are leaders of the believers in the city. His aunt Lydia for one," said Paul. "I think it would be good for you two to travel together."

More partings and more farewells took place as the two friends left Rome and headed east for Macedonia.

"Greet all our friends in Philippi," said Paul. "Tell them I hope to come as soon as I can."

Eighteen months passed. Paul stayed in Rome most of the time. He spent many hours teaching people of all backgrounds, both Jewish and Gentile. News came from friends and the assemblies of believers in the east from time to time as word spread in Macedonia, Achaia, and Asia that Paul was in Rome.

Paul developed a deep and warm relationship with Nereus and his sister Lucina. He started visiting Lucina regularly in her villa outside the city on the Via Ostiensis. Together, they talked for hours, and Paul shared with her some of his deepest hopes and also his struggles. One day he said to Lucina,

"I still have a deep and unfulfilled longing in my heart."

"Oh? Do you want to tell me about it?" probed Lucina.

"For years, I have wanted to take the message about Jesus to the farthest reaches of the empire in the west," said Paul.

"Hispania?" asked Lucina.

"Exactly, I am seriously thinking about going soon."

"Would it be wise to go all that way on your own? And what about the language? They don't speak Greek over there, you know. Are you sure this is what the Father is saying to you?"

"Absolutely," said Paul.

"You sound sure of yourself. It's not quite like you, Paul." There was a note of caution in her voice.

In the summer of his second year in Rome, Paul fulfilled his long-held wish. He undertook a visit to Hispania. Leaders among the Christians in Rome were not enthusiastic.

"The problem you will encounter, Paul, will be the language barrier," they told him. "Most locals speak ancient dialects, and the more educated classes speak Latin, which you have not yet mastered."

Paul could be stubborn at times, and this was one of them. He persuaded the young Corinthian, former slave, Apelles, to go with him. They returned some weeks later at the end of the summer.

When asked about his trip, all Paul would say was to quote the words of John the baptiser, 'A person can receive only what is given them from heaven.'

One day, as they sat sowing tents in their workshop, Priscilla asked him point blank. Apelles had dropped by to greet Paul and was there also.

"I take it, from what little you have said," she asked, "Hispania was not given you from heaven?"

CHAPTER XIV

"I'm still learning, Prisca," said Paul. "My plans are not always the Father's plans. My good ideas are just that, my good ideas. Amazingly, he blesses even my plans simply because he loves me and I am his son. But I am learning when it is what the Father is doing, there is fruit and a harvest. Even if it is hard and the journey long, when it is the Father's work, there is joy and fruit. I had no joy on my journey to Hispania. There was no fruit. Was there, Apelles?"

"You might think that, Paul. I couldn't possibly comment," said Apelles with a huge smile on his face.

One day a messenger arrived with a letter for Paul. It was news from Titus in Corinth. Paul was overjoyed to read of his friends in the city and how the community was growing and maturing under Titus' wise leadership. It also contained news of Titus' growing role as a leader in the area.

"Listen to this," said Paul to Priscilla and Aquila. "Titus has made a visit to the island of Crete. He spent several months there and reports there are communities of believers in several places across the island. He is wondering if he should move there to strengthen them."

"This is wonderful news," said Priscilla.

"I have a growing desire to go back to the east to visit the brothers there. What do you think?" asked Paul.

"I think this may well be the prompting of the Spirit," she said. "You will know, I'm sure. I'm learning the longings in our hearts are usually confirmed by other things too. This letter may be such a confirmation."

Paul wrote to Titus and encouraged him to go to Crete as soon as he could and finish the work he had begun there. He added that he hoped one day he would be able to visit him there.

Towards the end of his second year in Rome another letter arrived from the east, this time from Timothy who Paul had left in Ephesus. Reading the letter left Paul feeling troubled and concerned for his young friend.

"I think I may have more confirmation," Paul said the next day as he sat working with Priscilla and Aquila. "I received a letter from Timothy."

"Oh, how is he?" asked Aquila.

"Well, you know how he is. Don't you?" Paul said. "He is struggling, it seems. His health isn't too good. The community in Ephesus isn't thriving. He thinks the people are not as committed as he would like them to be. Everything seems hard work by the sound of things.

"So, anyway, I think this is the prompting I need," said Paul. "I have decided to go east again. I would like to revisit a number of the places we all know so well. It's almost been five years since I was last there.

"I am also thinking, maybe you two would consider returning to the east some time, particularly to Ephesus to support the brothers there and be an encouragement to Timothy. Please pray about it and let's keep in touch."

"What does Lucina think?" asked Priscilla.

"I haven't told her yet," Paul replied.

"Well, don't leave it too long before you do. She will miss you greatly. You do know this don't you, Paul?" Priscilla looked oddly at Paul.

CHAPTER XIV

"Err, Yes, of course I do," he replied with a confused look on his face.

Aquila looked at Paul equally confused. Priscilla looked from one to the other, and then shook her head.

"Men."

CHAPTER XV

Having made the decision to return for another visit to the communities in the east, particularly in Macedonia and Asia, Paul quickly formed his plans. He hoped to leave in the late summer before any sea travel would complicate his plans.

"The last thing I want is to add a fifth shipwreck to my list of troubles," he joked with Lucina.

Paul had been enjoying a few days of rest at her country estate outside the city. They were sitting under an awning in her extensive garden. It gently flapped in the breeze. The two sat for many hours enjoying the air and the scents of the garden and each other's company.

"I do wish you were not travelling alone, Paul. You are not as young as you used to be," Lucina said. "I will worry about you."

"There is no need to worry. Father is always with me."

"I know, but it doesn't change what I will be thinking about as long as you are away. My greatest concern is I might never see you again."

She wiped a tear from her eye hoping Paul would not see it.

A servant entered the garden and bowed before Lucina.

CHAPTER XV

"There are visitors, Lady. They ask to speak with you. They say their names are the Lady Priscilla and her husband Aquila."

"Welcome them into the house, we will come directly," said Lucina.

"I wonder why they are here," said Paul.

"I have no idea," said Lucina, hiding a smile.

They all greeted one another in the atrium and Lucina invited Priscilla and Aquila to sit with them in the garden. There was brief small talk, but it was obvious to Paul they had something they wanted to say.

"Paul," began Aquila, "we have given this a great deal of thought and we are determined in our minds this is God's will for us."

Paul looked at them wondering what was about to come.

"We believe we are meant to accompany you on your journey and to eventually return to Ephesus," said Priscilla.

Paul stood and covered his face with his hands. Then he stretched out his arms in a wide gesture to embrace them both.

A week later, a group of people gathered again at Lucina's house to bid farewell to the three travellers. Nereus was there, and a somewhat tearful Lucina, along with a few others.

"Send me news when you can, dear friends. I will be praying and longing to know you are safe," said Lucina through her tears.

Priscilla looked at Paul. A light had finally gone on in Paul's head.

"Yes! Err… Yes, of course we will," he said awkwardly.

Everyone gathered around Paul, Aquila and Priscilla and prayed for them and sent them on their way. Then, with a nudge from

Priscilla, he walked over to Lucina and hugged her, kissing her gently on her forehead.

∿∿∿

The three travellers left early the next day and took the Via Appia south in the direction of Puteoli as Paul had done in reverse over two years before. Messages had been sent to Junia, and also Julius, who came to meet them in Puteoli.

"I have found passage for you as you requested," he said. "It's a ship carrying a cargo of pumice and volcanic ash to Crete. Apparently, they use it in making waterproof concrete. There is a big building project underway in the harbour in Hierapytna on the southern coast of the island. With a fair wind, you should be there in about a week."

Paul, along with Priscilla and Aquila, embarked and set sail the next day waved off by many friends including Junia and Julius. Exactly a week later, the island of Crete appeared on the horizon after an uneventful journey. They made enquiries among the local Jewish community if they knew the whereabouts of any followers of the Nazarene. After a few days, word reached Titus and he joyously greeted them in Hierapytna.

Titus took them around the island introducing them to the scattered groups of believers. Deeply encouraged by their visit, he was sad when the three travellers announced their plans to cross over to the mainland before the summer sailing season came to an end and the unfavourable wind patterns returned. Before leaving, Paul gathered the believers together. He encouraged them to look to Titus as their leader and teacher.

CHAPTER XV

"This man standing before you is like a son to me." Paul rested his hand on Titus' shoulder.

"We have journeyed together over many years, and I commend him to you and before God to be a shepherd to you."

Paul embraced Titus and said, "I will send others to support you in the work here as soon as I can, dear boy."

Paul and his two friends found passage on a ship going to Ephesus and set sail on the next leg of their journey. As they sailed into the great harbour of Ephesus, Paul's mind went back to a previous time when he sailed into the harbour. As before, he could see the familiar skyline and the great Temple of Artimas dominating the city. He spotted the villa previously belonging to Onesiphorus' family, next to the Proconsul's palace. He wondered where Onesiphorus lived following his father's murder some years before.

The travellers docked and quickly made their way through the familiar streets to a house where they knew some believers lived. They were instantly recognised and welcomed. Messages were sent and within a short while, Timothy and Onesiphorus arrived. The joy at their reunion was immense. Timothy was totally overwhelmed and cried on Paul's shoulder, then switched to Priscilla where he cried even more.

Eventually, Timothy recovered, and they all sat down to drink wine and eat a meal.

"Tell us about everyone and all the news," said Paul. "We are eager to hear."

Timothy poured out a torrent of woes, which left them concerned and glad they had returned. Onesiphorus was more positive but struck a warning note.

"These are difficult days," he explained. "Since you left, the believers here have fragmented. Nowadays, we do not all gather together as there is some dissension and disagreements about some aspects of the gospel.

"Do you remember Hymenaeus?" he continued. "He was the chief steward of Apollonius the Asiach. He was always slightly non-committal and not totally with us in those early days. When Silanus was murdered, along with my father, the city's asiachs lost much of their authority, Apollonius included. Hymenaeus seized the opportunity to grab power. He rules over Apollonius' household and has some hold over Apollonius himself. He has effectively taken over the leadership of some of the groups of believers."

"Nothing I could say helped. He tried to undermine me and everything I did," added Timothy, who looked as if he would cry again.

Onesiphorus picked up the story.

"When Tychicus came with a letter from you over two years ago, Paul, at first, Hymenaeus said it wasn't from you. Then he said it wasn't addressed to the believers here in Ephesus, so he would not allow it to be read and accused you of teaching false truth. He is joined by a man called Philetus."

"Do you think it would help if I went to see them and talked to them?" Paul asked.

"It would be a start," said Timothy. "How long do you intend to stay, Paul?"

"I am not sure. But we have talked, and Aquila and Priscilla are going to remain here for the foreseeable future to support and encourage you."

CHAPTER XV

"This is really good news," said Timothy. His eyes welled up again.

"What about you, Onesiphorus? Do you have plans?" asked Paul.

"I have a desire to go to Rome and find my mother," he replied. "Do you remember she went to Rome with Silanus' widow when he and my father were killed? I have not heard from her for a long time, and I hope to go when I can leave my affairs in order here."

∿∿∿

In Ephesus, events unfolded quicker than Paul expected. Several of the local leaders did not welcome his return and Paul encountered strong opposition from two other leaders, Phygelus and Hermogenes, and then also from Hymenaeus and Philetus. They started spreading rumours about Paul and dug up the incident from several years ago which had resulted in a riot. One of the aggrieved traders, a believer named Alexander the coppersmith, was manipulated into opposing Paul whenever he spoke. It was a sad and sorry time for the believers in Ephesus.

Those who supported Paul felt his presence had provoked the situation and felt his life might be in danger if he stayed. They all agreed it would be best for Paul to go down the coast to Miletus and lodge there and await developments.

"I will stay there for the winter, and then I want to go to Macedonia, and on to Corinth when the weather improves," Paul said.

Paul went overland to Miletus having sent messages to a few of his friends throughout the region. For several months, Miletus became a hub of friends coming and going. Many had worked with Paul over a number of years, and they talked together about the spread of the good news of Jesus in the area. Trophimus arrived. Titus came from Crete. Tychicus came too, and Timothy, Aquila, Priscilla and Onesiphorus visited regularly from Ephesus.

Erastus came from Corinth in the early winter with concerning news from Rome.

"Apparently there has been a huge fire in Rome," Erastus reported. "I heard it at the governor's residence some weeks ago."

Concerned for many of his friends in the city, Aquila asked, "What do you mean *huge*?"

"It happened mid-summer when the weather is at its hottest," said Erastus.

"The city was sweltering in the summer heat with little rain for months. The fire began in the merchant shops around the Circus Maximus and burned uncontrolled for six days. It died down a bit but before the damage could be assessed, a strong wind reignited the fire and it burned for another three days."

"How awful," said Priscilla. "Do you know what part of the city was affected?"

"Mostly the suburra areas east and north of the forum. The report said two thirds of Rome has been destroyed," said Erastus.

Everyone was shocked at this news, knowing the fire likely affected homes and businesses of many of the believers.

"The emperor has sent messages to the provincial governors and Pro Consuls to send funds to help with the rebuilding," said Erastus. "I read the report. However, what particularly alarmed me was something about the cause of the fire. There are rumours Nero himself arranged for the fire to be started so he could build himself an enormous palace in the burnt section."

CHAPTER XV

"Where exactly?" asked Aquila.

"I can't remember the exact details," replied Erastus. "But three of Rome's fourteen districts were completely devastated; seven more were reduced to a few scorched and mangled ruins and only four completely escaped damage. The Temple of Jupiter, the house of the Vestals and part of Nero's palace were damaged or destroyed."

"But the worst news is people are reportedly saying Nero is blaming Christians for having started the fire."

"How ludicrous," said Aquila. "They would not start a fire. The emperor must be mad."

"I delayed coming here until I had more accurate details," added Erastus. "As soon as it arrived, I came here immediately. The emperor ordered the arrest of a few members of what is being referred to as the *Christian sect*. Under torture, they accused others until the entire Christian community has been implicated and became fair game for retribution."[65]

They listened in stunned silence as Erastus continued.

"As many as could be found were rounded up and have been put to death in the most horrific manner for the amusement of the citizens of Rome."

"Oh no," said Priscilla holding her hands to her face in shock.

"Shall I continue? It is so terrible," said Erastus.

"Continue, we must know what is going on," said Paul. "Prisca, do you want to hear this?"

She buried her head in Aquila's shoulder. "Yes, yes, we need to know the worst."

Erastus continued, "Nero used the believers for sport. He covered them in the skins of wild beasts and had them set upon by hungry dogs. Some, he nailed to crosses and covered them with pitch. Then he set fire to them to serve as lights in his own garden."[66]

"How many?" asked Paul.

"I don't know," said Erastus.

The friends sat in solemn silence as the enormity of this news sank in. They prayed and wept together and wondered what to do.

"We must send word to our brothers and sisters in Rome and find out what we can do," said Paul.

During the winter months, letters took longer to arrive, and it was in late winter before news finally came from Rome. Paul received a letter from Lucina. He broke the seal and unrolled the parchment. It was written in Lucina's own hand. Paul could not take in the horrors she related.

The number of names he recognised among those who suffered was deeply shocking. He wept as he read the letter. He sent word for Aquila and Priscilla to come as they would know these people too.

"Thank God at least Lucina is alive. Her brother, our dear friend, Nereus, has achieved the crown of righteousness. He was crucified and set alight in Nero's garden," said Paul.

"No! No! No!" moaned Priscilla.

"My dear friend, Ampliatus, Urbanus, my friend Stachys. Tryphena, Asyncritus, Phlegon, Patrobas, Hermas, Philologus, Julia, Olympas... The list goes on. Lucina says many of them were hiding in one of the catacombs outside the city and were betrayed.

"There is something even worse," Paul's voice choked as he tried

CHAPTER XV

to read. "Simon Peter was in Rome when all this happened, and he was arrested too and…"

Paul could not continue as he began to sob deeply. The scroll fell from his hands to the floor. Aquila picked it up and read its final section.

"He was taken outside the city across the river to the Campus Vaticanus where Nero races chariots," read Aquila slowly. "He was crucified there, apparently upside down."

The pain of this news weighed heavily on all of them.

∿∿∿

Spring returned and Paul resolved he would move on. His plan was to travel north to Troas by ship along the coast, cross into Macedonia and then down into Corinth. He had also resolved to return to Rome. No more reports of persecution had come, and he had written to Lucina to say he would return as soon as he was able.

Just as Paul was about to travel, Trophimus fell sick, too sick to travel any further, so he remained in Miletus. Titus was despatched back to Crete and Paul promised to send help as soon as he could. Tychicus accompanied Paul on his journey. Timothy, Onesiphorus, Aquila and Priscilla remained in Ephesus. Paul took a ship in Miletus and sailed up the coast of Asia to Troas where the ship docked.

Paul's arrival in Troas was a cause of great rejoicing for the believers in the city. It had been six years since his last memorable visit. Paul and Tychicus made their way through the streets to the house of Carpus.

The door was opened by a tall handsome man whose face beamed in delight when he recognised Paul.

"Eutychus," exclaimed Paul, "What has happened to you? Look at you! You were just a spotty boy last time I saw you."

"Thanks, Paul, nice of you to remind me," Eutychus replied grinning. "Come in, come in. Father is at home and there is someone else I want you to meet."

They went into the house and greeted Carpus. Eutychus came back leading a little boy by the hand who was about two years old. The child hung back with his arm around Eutychus' leg.

"Paul, I would like you to meet Paulus, my son. I named him after you," Eutychus said proudly.

They sat together and Carpus reported on all that had happened in the last six years.

"Oh! And of course, Lucas is here," said Carpus, "He came from Judaea a few months ago. He is staying with Demas. Eutychus, can you send someone to Demas' house and tell them Paul is here. They will be so pleased. I need to get food ready. We will be a merry crowd around the table here tonight."

Paul was thrilled to hear Lucas was in Troas. When he arrived an hour or so later, there was a warm reunion.

Paul shared all the news, including the tragic news from Rome. Word had started to spread around the Christian communities in the east of the events in Rome. The news resulted in shock and anxiety in most places as the implications sunk into people's hearts. The realisation was growing of the cost of being a follower of Jesus in a basically hostile world where life was cheap. The idea of taking up their cross as Jesus had done was no longer just a turn of phrase

CHAPTER XV

but a sobering reality.

"Tell me, Lucas, how are they in Caesarea? What news of Jerusalem and the brothers and sisters there?" Paul asked.

"Judaea is a tinderbox," said Lucas, "ready to catch fire any day. The Zealots are becoming increasingly bold in their methods and attacks on Romans and pro-Roman Jews. Porcius Festus died not long after we arrived in Rome, which explains why we didn't hear anything more about your case. However, the current governor, Gessius Florus, is one of Nero's cronies and has no understanding or sympathy for the Jews. I think it is just a matter of time before there is a full-scale rebellion."

"What of our friends in Caesarea?" Paul enquired.

"Sadly, Zacchaeus has passed into the arms of the Father," said Lucas. "Cornelius is one of the main leaders there now."

"And the second volume of your work? Is it complete?" asked Paul.

"Indeed, it is. I am rather pleased with it and my first volume about Jesus. I have copies of both here. I would love to show you."

∿∿∿

Time passed quickly in Troas. Paul commented it seemed to go much quicker now he was older. Before long, he was ready to move on, ever drawn to go west and make his way back to Rome. The group now included Lucas and Demas, who joined Paul and Tychicus. Without the manpower to take everything with them, Paul left his thick winter cloak and several parchments, among other things, with Carpus.

As in Troas, there were welcome reunions in Philippi. Paul was particularly interested to hear from Lydia about her nephew Lysias who had finally declared himself a follower of Jesus.

"He has gone back to Rome," Lydia said. "After news came of the horrors perpetrated on the brothers and sisters there, he felt he had to go see if he could help them. Apparently, there is a lady in Rome he is concerned for, a widow who survived the slaughter."

"Yes, indeed. That would be Lucina. I know her well," said Paul.

Lydia looked at him quizzically.

With a twinkle in her eye, she asked.

"Paul? Is there something you are not telling me?"

~~~~~~

The visit was short. Paul wanted to stop in Thessalonica and Berea and greet the community of believers in those cities, so they pressed on. He was also eager to eventually make his way to Corinth.

"I don't want to spend too long in Corinth," Paul said to Lucas. "I would like to get across to the other side of Achaia to Nicopolis and if necessary, spend the winter there. If it is mild and not too severe, we could even cross over to Brindisium and follow the via Appia to Rome from there. We will just have to see. I'm praying daily for our dear friends in Rome, and I am eager to go back."

Corinth was so familiar to Paul. He remembered the first time he came to the city almost fifteen years before. His last visit, five years before, he spent three months teaching and writing his letter to the Roman believers. Even as he thought about this, the longing to go back to Rome became greater.

CHAPTER XV

The four of them stayed in Erastus' house.

"I'm going to write to Titus and Timothy while I am here. After the visits we made, I feel there is much I want to remind them about. With Tychicus here we can get the letters done easily. He does well as an amanuensis. I don't know what I would have done over these years."

Paul began writing to Titus.

"My true son in our shared faith," he called him. "The reason I left you in Crete was that you might put in order what was left unfinished and appoint elders in every town as I directed you."[67]

The letter was full of practical instruction for all people in the community. Then Paul sat back and decided to put into simple words the essence of the gospel he and his team preached. It contained themes from all his previous letters.

"At one time we were foolish, disobedient, deceived and enslaved by all kinds of passions and pleasures. We lived in malice and envy, being hated and hating one another. But when the kindness and love of God our Saviour appeared, he saved us, not because of righteous things we had done, but because of his mercy. He saved us through the washing of rebirth and renewal by the Holy Spirit, whom he poured out on us generously through Jesus Christ our Saviour, so that, having been justified by his grace, we might become heirs having the hope of eternal life."[68]

Towards the end of the letter, Paul's mind went to practical things.

He had spoken with Artemas and Tychicus about going to Crete after Tychicus had taken the next letter he was about to write to Timothy in Ephesus. Paul saw the need to expand the leadership on Crete as he was thinking about asking Titus to join him before winter. He also had met with Apollos and another man called Zenas who were on their way east and would be stopping for a while in Crete.

"As soon as I send Artemas or Tychicus to you, do your best to come to me at Nicopolis. I have decided to winter there. Do everything you can to help Zenas the lawyer and Apollos on their way and see that they have everything they need."[69]

When the letter was complete, Paul said to Tychicus.

"Before we send this, I want to write to Timothy. It would be easier if you could carry the letters and go to Crete via Ephesus."

As soon as the letter to Titus was copied, Paul began writing to Timothy in Ephesus. His concern for Timothy was always in the forefront of his mind. Timothy was not emotionally strong and the challenges of leading a group of Christian believers was not something he enjoyed or managed well. As he did with Titus, Paul viewed Timothy as a son in the faith.

Paul urged Timothy to stay a while longer in Ephesus. Then he wrote,

"Timothy, my son, I am giving you this command in keeping with the prophecies once made about you, so that by recalling them you may fight the battle well, holding on to faith and a good conscience."[70]

As in the letter to Titus, Paul encouraged Timothy in his practical day to day dealings with people among the believers in Ephesus. He also thought about his ongoing battle with ill health.

One day when Lucas had come to visit, Paul asked the doctor,

"What can I say to Timothy about his constant tummy troubles?"

CHAPTER XV

"Tell him to stop drinking the water," said Lucas. "He doesn't listen to me on that one. Maybe he will listen to you, Paul. Tell him to drink wine instead. Everyone knows the water in summer gets bad."

"Stop drinking only water and use a little wine because of your stomach and your frequent illnesses. How does that sound?" asked Paul.[71]

"Perfect, just the sort of thing I would say," said Lucas grinning.

Nearly finished with the letter, Paul contemplated how to end it. Then he said to Tychicus,

"Write this please, 'But you, man of God, flee from all this, and pursue righteousness, godliness, faith, love, endurance, and gentleness. Fight the good fight of the faith. Take hold of the eternal life to which you were called when you made your good confession in the presence of many witnesses.'"[72]

A few days later, the letters had been copied and Tychicus and Artemas were ready to set off for Ephesus. Demas, who had travelled from Troas with Paul, finally told Paul he would not be going to Rome with him but wanted to return home via Thessalonica.

"Why don't you come with us to Rome?" asked Lucas.

"I don't want to go to Rome. I don't want to be a martyr," Demas said petulantly. "From what we keep hearing, Paul is going to walk right into a situation where people are being arrested and killed. I don't intend to be one of them. I think you are foolish to go with him."

Both Lucas and Paul were shocked and surprised by his attitude.

"Let him go," said Paul. "There is no point in trying to

persuade him."

"Come, Lucas, let us go on while it is still not winter," said Paul. "We can head north and west over the mountains to Nicopolis. If the winter sets in early, we can stay there for a few months. There is a large Jewish community in the city and there may even be followers of Jesus there already."

"Didn't you ask Titus to join us in Nicopolis?" Lucas asked.

"Yes, I did. But if the weather is favourable and we can cross over to Italy, I want to take the opportunity it affords. If Titus does not arrive before we leave, we can leave a message there for him."

"So, the weather is guiding you now is it, Paul? What is the Spirit saying?" asked Lucas.

Paul looked askance.

"You know I am longing to get to Rome. Don't pressure me like this," retorted Paul as he got up to leave the room.

Erastus came to see Paul and told him he also was not going to Rome.

"I have responsibilities which keep me here in Corinth," said Erastus.

"I will send news to you in Rome. And, if Titus or Timothy come through Corinth, I will be able to help them on their way."

Paul and Lucas bade farewell to the many friends in Corinth and headed off for Nicopolis.

"May Father go with you, dear friends," said Erastus to Paul and Lucas.

He had accompanied them as far as the city gate. Erastus had a

CHAPTER XV

dark sense of foreboding in his heart.

"Who knows when we will meet again," he said.

"Father knows," said Paul. "Either here or in his eternal arms."

Paul and Lucas both embraced Erastus and began the journey west.

They made a relatively quick journey across the mountains to Nicopolis. As Paul had hoped, the sailing season had not yet ended in the southern part of the Adriatic, and they easily found a ship which was going all the way to the newly built port of Ostia at the mouth of the River Tiber.

Paul was delighted, as this would shorten the journey and save many days walking along the main Via Appia to Rome. Rome was just twenty-five miles away from Ostia along the Via Ostiensis. They would then go straight to Lucina's house outside the city.

CHAPTER XVI

The ship entered the great new port of Ostia at the mouth of the River Tiber. As the main base of the Roman navy, the port was already packed with merchant ships and a large number of naval galleys, both biremes and triremes. A huge Imperial sailing ship was also berthed along the quay, while countless other smaller crafts dotted around the harbour.

"I have been in many harbours, and I have never seen so many ships all in one place in my entire life," said Paul.

"When we disembark, I presume we head straight to Rome along the Via Ostiensis?" asked Lucas.

"Yes, I think we must go to Lucina's villa first as it is outside the city. We can assess the situation once we get there," said Paul. "We need to be careful; we do not want to put any lives at risk by our presence in the city."

"Lucina will be grieving the death of her brother I am sure," said Lucas, "and we don't know how many others of our friends in the city had received the martyr's crown. All the rumours and reports are horrific."

The two friends walked along the crowded road to the city which followed the banks of the Tiber. Long teams of mules pulled heavily

CHAPTER XVI

laden barges along the river. New building work was everywhere along the road with huge warehouses being erected to house the vast supply of cargo and goods coming into the largest city in the world. Armies of slaves were everywhere. Paul realised again the desperate need of these wretched people and how the good news of Jesus would bring freedom to their spirits if not their physical bodies.

As they approached the outskirts of the city, they noticed areas of makeshift housing on all sides.

"I would think this must be where many of those who lost property and their homes are now living while things are rebuilt within the walls," commented Lucas.

They passed the fifth milestone, then the fourth and third, and then they saw the second milestone along the road. Lucas noticed how Paul's pace quickened with each passing milestone. Lucina's house came into view on the slightly higher ground above the floodplain of the river. It looked the same as the last time they had seen it.

They approached the gates, which were shut, and banged on the door. A doorkeeper they did not recognise quickly appeared.

"What do you want?" asked the man somewhat suspiciously.

"Is the Lady Lucina at home?" asked Paul.

Even more guarded, he asked, "Who wants to know and what is your business with her?"

"We seek the welfare of the Lady. My name is Paul, and this is Lucas."

"Is she expecting you? Did you let her know you were coming?" he asked.

"Friend," said Paul, "we have travelled a long way and have just arrived this day at Ostia from Corinth. We have not had time to send a message. We are the message."

"Wait here." He shut the door in their faces.

"It seems the troubles our brothers and sisters have experienced this last year have made people anxious and wary," said Lucas. "I guess it is not surprising."

Paul and Lucas waited for quite a few minutes, and then they heard loud footsteps running towards the gate followed by a rattling of keys and bolts on the inside. Finally, they heard a familiar voice.

"Come on, man! Help me get these wretched bolts open, damn it."

When the door flung open, Lysias burst out into the road.

"Paul! Lucas! Is it really you?" shouted Lysias.

They all hugged and embraced one another with great joy.

"We had no idea you were coming," he said. "We would have come to meet you if we had known. But come in, get out of the road. It is not safe out here."

"What do you mean not safe?" asked Lucas.

"We are sure the house is being watched these days, ever since the fire and the beginning of the attacks on us," said Lysias. "Come in, come in. Lucina is at home. She was resting, but her maid has gone to wake her."

"Is she well?" asked Paul, unable to hide the anxiety in his voice.

"Yes, she is well. But she is not strong," said Lysias. "The trauma and the loss of Nereus has aged her. But see for yourself, here she comes."

Paul and Lucas turned and looked towards the portico along the

CHAPTER XVI

front of the house. The diminutive figure of Lucina slowly descended the steps. Paul walked towards her with his arms outstretched. They fell into each other's arms and wept.

The reunion for all four of them was bittersweet. They rejoiced in seeing each other and knowing each other was safe. Yet at the same time, the loss of so many friends and the suffering of the survivors and the relatives of those who had died for their faith was deeply painful.

Lucina led Lucas and Paul out into the garden to a quiet corner where she showed them a newly inscribed stone.

"This is where I buried what was left of my dear bother," she said softly.

They stood for a long time looking at the inscription with Nereus' name on the stone.

Paul ran his finger along the stone. "What is this symbol below his name, Lucina?"

"It is the sign of the fish. Many of us use it as sign to our friends to show we are believers. It is an acrostic," Lucina said.

"The Greek word for fish is 'ichthys'," said Lysias. "Each letter represents a word."

Paul and Lucas looked slightly bemused by this.

"Let me explain," said Lysias. "The letter 'Iota' is the first letter of the word 'Iesous'; 'chi' is the first letter of the word 'Christos'; 'theta' is the first letter of the word 'theou'; 'ypsilon' is the first letter of the word 'yuios' and 'sigma' is the first letter of the word 'soter'.

Paul and Lucas looked at him in amazement. Lysias continued.

"Put it all together, Iesous, Christos, Theou, Huios, Soter. 'Jesus Christ God's Son Saviour!' It spells the word Ichthys, and we Christians all know what it means. As far as we know, the authorities have not worked it out yet."

"This is incredible," said Lucas, "Whoever thought it up must be absolutely brilliant."

"He is, and he is far too modest to tell you himself," said Lucina smiling warmly at Lysias. "I can't say what a support and comfort Lysias has been to us all since he came back to Rome."

For once, Lysias looked slightly embarrassed.

"Come, let us go inside and find you somewhere to sleep," said Lucina. "The house is rather crowded these days. Some who lost their homes in the fire or have fled the city in fear of their lives are here with me. Several of Nereus' household are here helping with the extra work."

"When Nereus was seized and martyred," said Lysias, "his house was taken by the Emperor. A rich senator, whose villa on the Caelian Hill was destroyed in the fire, petitioned Caesar to requisition the property claiming it belonged to one of the so-called instigators. Nero saw this as an opportunity to make money and sold it to the senator. Of course, not a denarius went to Nereus' family. Ever since then, Nero has been particularly interested in finding property owned by Christians."

"No wonder the doorkeeper was suspicious," said Lucas.

"Nero's lust for money has stretched far beyond his attacks on us," said Lysias. "Anyone he thinks is against him, or he considers a traitor, is at risk. There have been a number of conspiracies exposed at the heart of the senate and among the most noble and wealthy

CHAPTER XVI

of the city. Even the great patrician and senator Piso was recently accused and ordered to commit suicide along with a host of others.

"Many other conspirators have been executed. No one is safe anymore. Fear stalks the city and there are rumours the plebs, the hoi polio, have sympathy for the treatment and suffering dealt to the Christians. They say it is done just to satisfy one man's lust."

"It sounds as if Nero is no longer popular among the people," said Paul. "All the more reason for him to hear the good news about Jesus Christ, God's Son, the Saviour."

Lucina looked at Paul somewhat startled.

"What do you mean, Paul? Surely you don't plan to…" Her voice trailed off.

Over the following days, Paul and Lucas accompanied Lysias into the city where they visited a few homes of the believers. Many had moved across the river into the crowded suburb of Trastevere, so Lucas and Paul walked through this section of the city.

"This is where many Jews live," commented Paul. "I came here on many occasions when I was last in the city."

They met several friends who shared the struggles and losses of the last few months with them. It became apparent the once vibrant community of believers in the city was traumatised by the attacks on its members. Many had left the city and gone to friends and family in the countryside or to other cities. Reports emerged of a spread of the good news about Jesus as a result of the persecution.

One day a visitor arrived at Lucina's house. To Paul's delight, it was Onesiphorus.

"I have been in Rome for some time and have been looking

for you everywhere," said Onesiphorus. "No one wants to tell me anything about anyone in the city. It took me an age to locate my mother."

"How is she? Is she well?" asked Lucas.

"Yes, she is well," answered Onesiphorus. "She lives in a quiet part of the city with her friend Antonia Domitilla, the widow of Silanus. They live as quietly as they can as dignified Roman matrons and widows. They are both believers in Jesus but keep out of the public eye. They managed to avoid being swept up in Nero's attack on the family of God in the city."

A message came from Titus. He had gone to Nicopolis as Paul urged him to do and waited there until he heard more news. When Paul thought about Titus' situation, he decided to encourage him to remain in the area and to go and visit the communities in Dalmatia and further up the coast in Illyricum.

The only one Paul continually worried about was Timothy. He began to think Timothy would be better situated if he came to Rome rather than remain in Ephesus. The community in Ephesus were better served by Aquila and Priscilla than the fragile Timothy. With these various thoughts in mind, Paul started to write again to Timothy.

"Night and day I constantly remember you in my prayers. Recalling your tears, I long to see you, so that I may be filled with joy."[73]

The overall tone of the letter suggested Paul was seeing the end of an era in many ways. He reiterated the commissioning Timothy had received.

"For this reason, I remind you to fan into flame the gift of God,

CHAPTER XVI

which is in you through the laying on of my hands. For the Spirit God gave us does not make us timid, but gives us power, love, and self-discipline.

"What you heard from me, keep as the pattern of sound teaching, with faith and love in Christ Jesus. Guard the good deposit that was entrusted to you, guard it with the help of the Holy Spirit who lives in us.[74]

"In the presence of God and of Christ Jesus, who will judge the living and the dead, and in view of his appearing and his kingdom, I give you this charge: Preach the word; be prepared in season and out of season; correct, rebuke, and encourage, with great patience and careful instruction. For the time will come when people will not put up with sound doctrine. Instead, to suit their own desires, they will gather around them a great number of teachers to say what their itching ears want to hear. They will turn their ears away from the truth and turn aside to myths. But you, keep your head in all situations, endure hardship, do the work of an evangelist, discharge all the duties of your ministry."[75]

Paul paused to reflect on what he felt was about to happen to him.

"For I am already being poured out like a drink offering, and the time for my departure is near. I have fought the good fight, I have finished the race, I have kept the faith. Now there is in store for me the crown of righteousness, which the Lord, the righteous Judge, will award to me on that day and not only to me, but also to all who have longed for his appearing."[76]

Paul finished the letter in his customary way of sending news and greetings to his many friends in Ephesus from people in Rome who he thought Timothy might know.

"Do your best to come to me quickly, for Demas, because he loved this world, has deserted me and has gone to Thessalonica. Crescens has gone to Galatia, and Titus to Dalmatia. Only Luke is with me. Get Mark and bring him with you. He is helpful to me in my ministry. I sent Tychicus to Ephesus. When you come, bring the cloak that I left with Carpus at Troas, and my scrolls, especially the parchments.

"Greet Priscilla and Aquila and the household of Onesiphorus. Erastus stayed in Corinth, and I left Trophimus sick in Miletus. Do your best to get here before winter."[77]

Paul concluded the letter, and a copy was made to be kept by the believers in Rome. Onesiphorus had announced he would be returning to Ephesus in a few weeks and volunteered to take the letter.

The whole city seemed like a vast building site. There were still areas where entire insulae were nothing but blackened ruins. But the industrious Romans were also rebuilding everywhere. The Circus Maximus, where it was believed the fire had started, was still unfinished but chariot races had resumed quickly. One day, Paul, Lysias and Lucas walked around the eastern end of the Circus and ahead of them they saw a huge building being constructed covering almost the whole side of the Caelian Hill.

"They call it Nero's golden house,'" said Lysias. "All the money being sent to rebuild Rome from the provinces is going into this grand design of one man's vanity."

"Who is this?" asked Lucas pointing at a monumentally tall naked statue of a man.

"It is the 'beloved' emperor himself," said Lysias. "The colossus

CHAPTER XVI

of Nero. Some say it represents the sun god. It is being covered in beaten gold."

"He certainly has an inflated ego," said Lucas wryly.

"It is not the only thing about it that is inflated," sniggered Lysias.

Paul gazed at the grotesque statue of Nero. "It reminds me of a story in the Jewish scriptures. The Prophet Daniel interpreted a dream of King Nebuchadnezzar of Babylon in which he saw a huge statue, not dissimilar to this one, a man-made statue representing the king. Daniel saw it crumble and fall as it had feet of clay. It represented the King's narcissistic character. A rock struck the statue and it fell to the ground. Daniel told the king,

'The God of heaven will set up a kingdom that will never be destroyed, nor will it be left to another people. It will crush all those kingdoms and bring them to an end, but it will itself endure forever.'[78]

"This scripture prefigures the coming of Jesus and his proclamation of the kingdom of God. We may be challenged today by the empire of Rome, but the Roman empire will fall before the kingdom of our God and of his anointed son. At his name every knee shall bow, in heaven and on earth and under the earth, and every tongue acknowledge that Jesus Christ is Lord, to the glory of God the Father."

Lucas and Lysias looked at Paul whose eyes were fixed on the shining head of the statue of Nero.

"I have an appointment to keep with this man with feet of clay. You remember when we were in the storm before we were shipwrecked on Malta, an angel of the Lord appeared to me. He told me, 'Do not be afraid, Paul. You must stand trial before Caesar.'

Now I know what I have to say to him. It is just a matter of time before I get the opportunity."

"Paul, you know what this means, don't you?" said Lysias. "In this current climate, it will mean arrest and most probably, certain death."

"Yes, I know," said Paul. "I will put all my affairs in order, and then I will seek an audience with him."

"How do you intend to do that?" asked Lucas.

"The senator who took Nereus' house," said Paul. "He may hold another key to get me into Nero's presence. We shall see."

Arrests of Christians had virtually stopped, and many hoped the worst was over as people got on with rebuilding their lives, their homes, and the city. In the following days, Paul spent a lot of time praying and talking with his close friends. Lucas detected a different tone in Paul's manner since returning to Rome. Paul was quiet and seemed focused on finding a way to gain access to the emperor.

Lucas sat with Paul one day and asked him what he felt was his next step.

"Ever since I saw the statue of Nero among the ruins of the fire," Paul answered, "I have felt strongly I should try to speak to him. My plan had been to write the letter to Timothy, which I have done. As I said in the letter, 'the time for my departure is near. I have fought the good fight, I have finished the race, I have kept the faith.' I am resolved to go to see Nero," Paul said firmly. "I don't want you or Lysias or anyone trying to stop me."

"But how will you do it?" asked Lucas.

"I am going to the man who stole Nereus' house. He is a friend

CHAPTER XVI

of Nero. I will make him take me to the emperor. I don't want you or anyone else coming with me. Is that clear?"

The next day, Lucina, Lysias and Lucas were talking.

"There is no dissuading him," said Lucas. "When Paul has made up his mind, he can be remarkably stubborn.

"We may not go with him, but we can follow him from a distance and see what happens," suggested Lysias.

"Whatever happens," said Lucina, "bring him back here to me."

Early the next morning, Paul got up thinking the whole house was asleep. He walked quietly down to the gate. In the darkness of the portico, two figures dressed in dark cloaks stood watching. Paul went through the gate and the two figures left the villa and went out through the gate after him.

Lysias and Lucas followed from a distance keeping a close eye on Paul as he entered the city. His route took him up to the Aventine Hill and soon they turned into the street where Nereus' house was. They ducked into a doorway and watched as Paul banged on the door. The doorkeeper opened the door and after some discussion, he was admitted into the house.

Lysias and Lucas waited several hours. People came and went, but there was no sign of Paul.

"Listen," said Lysias. "I hear the sound of soldiers approaching."

As he spoke, a troop of praetorian guards came up the street and stopped at the door. Within a few minutes, Paul, bound with his hands behind his back, was escorted out of the house accompanied by the patrician dressed in his senatorial toga.

The senator led the soldiers and Paul down the hill towards the

Circus Maximus. They took the road through the Forum Boarium between the Palatine Hill and the Capitoline Hill. The soldiers stopped outside the Mamertine prison adjacent to the Forum and Paul was roughly pushed into the cell. They watched as a guard was placed outside the prison. Then the senator and captain of the Praetorians left and headed across the forum to the Imperial Palace.

"Why would they put him in the Mamertine prison?" asked Lucas.

"It is not good news," said Lysias. "It is used for housing prisoners under a death sentence. Usually, they are taken and thrown off the Tarpian Rock. See it up there on the side of the hill next to the Temple of Jupiter."

Lysias and Lucas waited all day in the Forum. Late in the evening, soldiers came from the palace and Paul was taken across the Forum to the main entrance of the palace. Lysias and Lucas followed but could not go into the palace itself. Lights burned high up in the upper rooms of the palace. The two must have waited about two hours.

They were sitting on the steps of the Temple of Castor and Pollux nodding off when a sound woke them up.

"Look, someone is coming," said Lysias. "It's not soldiers, they look like slaves to me."

A group of slaves were leaving the palace carrying a linen bundle.

They headed in the direction of the river.

"Come on, quickly!" said Lysias.

The two friends caught up with the slaves, who were alarmed as the two men who ran up to them.

"What are you carrying?" demanded Lysias.

CHAPTER XVI

Frightened, the slaves dropped the bundle. Lysias grabbed one of the men by the arm.

"Tell me. What is this?" Lysias looked at the blood-soaked linen bundle.

"Just carrying out orders, sir," the slave said. "It's just some prisoner. He was talking with Nero, and he angered the emperor. He had him beheaded on the spot. We were told to dispose of the body in the river."

"Your job is done, leave it to us," said Lucas.

Lucas knelt and started to pull back the linen.

"No! Don't, Lucas. You don't want to see it," whispered Lysias.

"I have to. I have to know for sure. I have to know it is him," replied Lucas shacking off Lysias' hand.

"Aaaah! No! No! No!" cried Lucas as he fell back in shock at the sight of the familiar blood soaked tunic and the severed head of his dear friend.

The first rays of the sun were beginning to appear across the sky and with it, the daily traffic of the wakening city. Lysias stopped a passing man with a hand cart and engaged him. Carefully, they picked up the body of Paul in the linen bundle and headed out of the city along the Via Ostiensis. They stopped in front of Lucina's house at the second milestone and paid off the cart driver.

Lucas ran ahead calling for assistance, while Lysias picked up the bundle and lovingly carried it in his arms. He walked slowly up to the house. Many of the household came out with Lucina. She fell to her knees weeping as Lysias approached carrying his precious bundle.

"Come, I have a place prepared for him," said Lucina. "Follow me."

Lucas helped her to her feet, and she led them through the house into the garden to the quiet place where Nereus was buried. A grave had been freshly dug and awaited the earthly remains of one of greatest men the world would ever see.[79]

Lysias carefully placed Paul's body in the grave. Together with Lucas, they covered it over with the fresh earth.

"Here lies Paul of Tarsus, an apostle of the Lord Jesus Christ by the will of God. Rest in peace in the Father's arms, my dear friend." said Lucina.

POSSIBLE ROUTE OF PAUL'S LAST JOURNEY

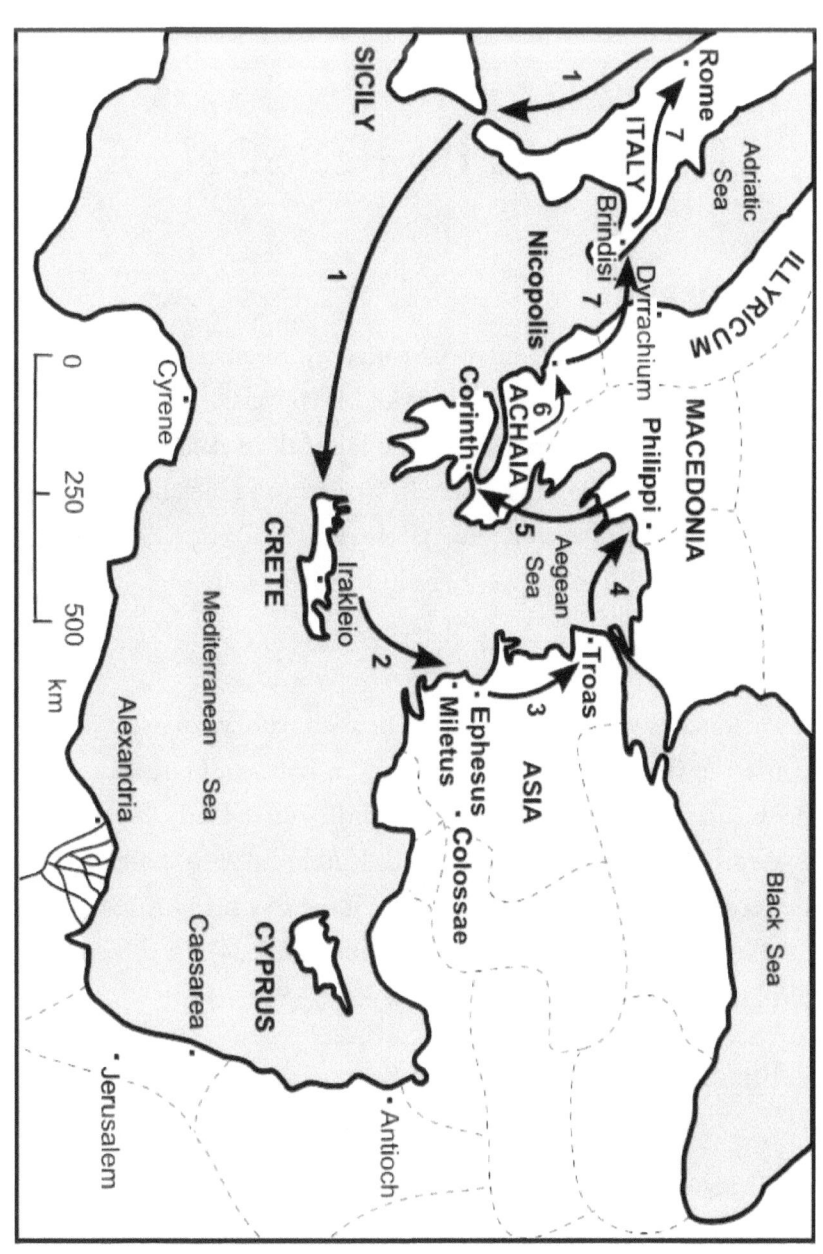

DRAMATIS PERSONAE

Apelles

Apelles was one of the many Christians in Rome referenced in the last chapter of Romans. Paul knew of his conversion and described him as having been tested and found faithful. In *Paul – the Middle Years*, I placed Apelles' conversion in Corinth, and then he is encouraged to go to Rome by Chloe (Romans 16:10). In this story, he accompanied Paul on a possible trip to Spain.

Aristarchus

Aristarchus was a Thessalonica Christian who was likely a Jewish convert to Christianity. He visited Paul in Ephesus. During the riot, he was seized by an angry mob toward the end of Paul's long stay in Ephesus. He ended up in prison with Paul in Ephesus. Luke tells us he accompanied Paul on the fateful journey by sea to Rome (Acts 19:29, 20:4, 27:2; Colossians 4:10; Philemon 1:24). In this story, I left him on Malta assisting the believers on the island.

Berenice

Berenice of Cilicia, also known as Julia Bernice, was a Jewish queen. She was the daughter of King Herod Agrippa I and a sister of King Herod Agrippa II. She is mentioned in the Acts of the

Apostles (25:13, 23; 26:30). She spent much of her life at the court of her brother Herod Agrippa II, amidst rumours the two were carrying on an incestuous relationship. During the First Jewish-Roman War, she began a love affair with the future emperor Titus Flavius Vespasianus.

Claudius Lysias

Claudius Lysias was "the tribune of the cohort" in Jerusalem, stationed in nearby "barracks" (Acts 21:34, 37; 22:24, 23:10, 16, 32). The "barracks" referenced in the book of Acts (21:34, 37; 22:24; 23:10, 16, 32), are references to the Tower of Antonia, which Herod the Great rebuilt from a previous structure and named after Marc Antony. The Antonia was added onto the northwest side of the Temple facilities, "from which stairs descend into the outer court of the temple" (Acts 21:32, 35, 22:30). For this reason, the Roman Tribune could hear the commotion caused by the confusing riot over Paul's presence in the Temple, and respond with speed (Acts 21:27-32). His brief entry into the New Testament story left lots of possible lines of enquiry. I chose to make him part of the fictional thread throughout the book.

Cleopas

The only mention of Cleopas in the Bible is in Luke 24:18. Cleopas was one of two disciples Jesus met on the road to Emmaus on the day of His resurrection. We do not know the identity of the other disciple, but we know that neither was one of the eleven apostles remaining after Judas' death (verse 33). Cleopas and the other disciple were on the road to Emmaus, discussing the crucifixion and the empty tomb, when Jesus suddenly joined them, although they did not recognize him. The whole incident is described in

Luke 24:13–35. The fact that Luke recorded the name of Cleopas, who was not significant in any other way, probably indicates that Cleopas was Luke's source when writing of this incident. Cleopas and his traveling companion were some of the first to see Jesus after His resurrection.

Cornelius

Cornelius was a centurion in the Cohort II Italica Civium Romanorum, mentioned as *Cohors Italica* in the Vulgate. He was stationed in Caesarea Maritima, the capital of the Roman province of Judaea. He is depicted in the New Testament as a God-fearing man. His conversion is detailed in Acts 10. *The Apostolic Constitutions* (c375AD) say that the first Bishop of Caesarea was Zacchaeus the Tax Collector, followed by Cornelius (possibly Cornelius the Centurion) and Theophilus (possibly the one addressed in the Gospel of Luke). For this reason, I included him in the story in Caesarea.

Demas

Paul initially considered Demas a fellow labourer in the gospel. He was in Ephesus during Paul's imprisonment. A few years later, however, in his last letter to Timothy, Paul lamented that Demas forsook him to pursue what the world had to offer (Colossians 4:14; Philemon 1:24; II Timothy 4:10).

Erastus

Erastus is recorded three times in the New Testament. It is unclear, however, whether all these references are to the same person. I have concluded they are. In the Letter to the Romans, written from Corinth, Erastus is described as the city treasurer who sends greetings to the Romans. He visited Paul during his extended stay in Ephesus and was sent by him along with Timothy ahead into Macedonia to help encourage the churches in the area. The final time the name Erastus is mentioned is in II Timothy, where it is stated he was living in Corinth at the time of the letter (Acts 19:22; Romans 16:23; II Timothy 4:20).

Felix

Antonius Felix, a Greek freedman, was the fourth Roman procurator of Judea Province in 52–60, in succession to Ventidius Cumanus. Felix was the younger brother of the Greek freedman Marcus Antonius Pallas. Pallas served as a secretary of the treasury during the reign of the Emperor Claudius. Felix became the procurator by the petition of his brother. Felix's cruelty, coupled with his accessibility to bribes (Acts 24:26), led to a great increase of crime in Judaea. The period of his rule was marked by internal feuds and disturbances, which he put down with severity. On at least one occasion, Felix and his wife Drusilla heard Paul speak, and later on, frequently sent for Paul and talked with him. However, his actual desire was to receive a bribe from Paul.

Herod Agrippa II

Herod Agrippa (AD 27/28 – c. 92 or 100AD), was the last ruler from the Herodian dynasty, reigning over territories outside of Judea as a Roman client king. Agrippa II fled Jerusalem in 66, fearing the Jewish uprising and supported the Roman side in the First Jewish–Roman War. It was before Agrippa and his sister Berenice that, according to the New Testament, Paul the Apostle pleaded his case at Caesarea Maritima, probably in 59 or 60 (Acts 26).

DRAMATIS PERSONAE

James

The half-brother of Jesus, along with Jude, Joses, and Simon. James, as well as his brother Jude, wrote New Testament books named after them. Paul wrote that James, Jesus' brother, had a personal resurrection encounter with Jesus. Paul, after spending three years in Arabia, met James when he visited Jerusalem. Paul talked with James who presided over the Jerusalem conference in 49 A.D. Paul presumably met him in Jerusalem at the end of his second missionary journey, and then again at the end of his third missionary journey and before his arrest (Matthew 13:55, Mark 6:3, Galatians 1:19; Acts 12:17, 15:13, 21:18; I Corinthians 15:7; Galatians 1:19, 2:9, 12). In this story, I imagined James accompanying Luke to Galilee and introducing him to his mother, Mary.

John Mark

The cousin of Barnabas, Mark was a Jewish convert and writer of the Gospel named after him. His mother, called Mary, owned a house in Jerusalem with a large upstairs room. Mark travelled with Barnabas and Paul on their first missionary journey but left them when they got to Perga. Barnabas wanted to give Mark another chance and take him on the next journey, however, Paul refused to do so. Their disagreement was so serious that they separated. Years later, Paul reconciled to Mark. While in prison in Ephesus, the apostle sent a greeting from Mark to the church at Colossae. Paul also told Philemon that he considered Mark a fellow labourer. Around 64 to 65 A.D., Peter wrote that Mark was with him during his evangelism of "Babylon", which may have been code for Rome. In the last letter to Timothy, written in perhaps 67 A.D., Mark is listed as one of the few remaining people loyal to the apostle. Paul encouraged his friend to bring Mark to Rome "because he is helpful to me for the ministry of the Word" (Acts 12:12, 25, 15:37 - 39; Colossians 4:10; Philemon 1:24; I Peter 5:13; II Timothy 4:11).

Julius

Julius was a centurion of the Augustan Regiment of the Roman Army who was in charge with escorting Paul and other prisoners from Judea to Rome. During a gale, Paul was told by an angel of God that he was going to save all of the lives aboard the ship, although their ship would be destroyed; Paul exhorted all of the 276 men aboard the ship to have courage and run aground on some island. The soldiers planned to massacre the prisoners rather than let them escape, but Julius wanted to spare Paul's life and prevented the soldiers from carrying out their plan (Acts 27:1,3,43). In this story, I imagined Julius being so impressed by Paul's testimony he becomes a Christian. I also placed him as growing up in Pompeii. He visited his family and discovered a community of believers in the city, which is borne out by archaeological evidence and the work of Longenecker.

Junia

Junia, whose name follows Andronicus indicating she is his wife, is a woman greeted in the last chapter of Romans. According to Paul, she had been a Christian longer than he had and may have been his relative. He also mentions that she, along with her husband, had been in prison like Paul. Romans 16 also states Junia was "of note among the apostles." In the story, I placed both husband and wife as having an apostolic ministry in Rome (Romans 16:7). After becoming a widow, I placed her in Puteoli.

Lucas (Luke)

Luke was a Gentile convert who wrote the Gospel bearing his name and is the author of the Acts of the Apostles. Interestingly, he never mentions his own name anywhere in Acts. His signature is the 'we' passages where he includes himself in the action. Although his role in the church's early history was important, he is only referenced by name three times in the New Testament. He is affectionately referred to as "the beloved physician" by Paul. Luke travelled with Paul on parts of his second and third missionary journeys. (Colossians 4:14; Philemon 1:24) He also accompanied the apostle from Caesarea to Rome in 62 A.D. Luke arrived in Jerusalem with Paul. This section begins and ends with 'we' passages (Acts 21:17 – 19; Acts 27:1 – 2). In this story, I imagined he spent the two years of Paul's imprisonment in Caesarea meeting eyewitnesses to the life of Jesus and writing down their stories. Luke is again with Paul in 67 A.D. during his final days in Rome (II Timothy 4:11).

Lucina

This woman is not mentioned at all in the New Testament. However, there is an intriguing early tradition that mentions her. According to the *Liber Pontificalis,* a Roman Catholic book dating from the eighth or ninth century, Paul's body "was buried outside the walls of Rome, at the second mile on the Via Ostiensis, on the estate owned by a Christian woman named Lucina." On this slim piece of evidence, I built a "love interest" into the story.

Mary

The Mother of Jesus. In Luke's Gospel, he recounts very detailed stories surrounding the birth of Jesus. Nearly all scholars see her hand in the Luke stories. I have incorporated a personal visit to Mary by Luke (Luke 1- 3).

Mnason

A Jewish convert originally from Cyprus, Mnason lived in Jerusalem and provided hospitality to a number of people (Acts 21:17).

Nereus

He is one of the people greeted by Paul in his letter to the Romans (Romans 16:15). In the story, I placed him and his unnamed sister in Rome. I imagined his sister to be the woman Lucina.

Onesiphorus

Onesiphorus was a Christian who lived in Ephesus. He greatly aided the Apostle Paul during his first visit to the city. In the story, I connected him to Paul on a ship going from Corinth to Ephesus. I imagined him to be the son of one of Ephesus' asiachs. I created a fictitious father called Cassander and a mother called Julia Lavinia. Paul specially commended Onesiphorus for tracking him down and visiting him during his final stay in Rome. Onesiphorus frequently refreshed the apostle and was not ashamed of his chains, unlike so many others who appeared to abandon him (II Timothy 1:16 - 18, 4:19).

Peter, Simon Peter, (Cephas)

Peter was one of the original twelve apostles. He wrote two letters in the New Testament. He and Paul met three times during their ministries. When Paul journeyed to Jerusalem in 36 A.D., he stayed with Peter for fifteen days. When Paul, Barnabas and Titus went to Jerusalem in 49 A.D. for the council, Paul talked with Peter and some of the other apostles. Soon after this, Peter visited Antioch. During the first part of his visit, Peter readily mixed and ate with both Jewish and Gentile converts. When believing Pharisees visited from Jerusalem who believed Gentiles should adopt Jewish religious practices, he changed his behaviour. Peter's behaviour put him on a collision course with Paul, who was called to be the apostle to the Gentiles. Paul publicly rebuked him. In Peter's second letter written around 66 A.D, he acknowledged the truth written in Paul's letters and considered them on the same level of inspiration as Scripture (Galatians 1:18, 2:7 - 14; I Corinthians 1:12, 3:22, 9:5, 15:5; II Peter 3:15 – 16). In this story, I imagined Peter met Luke and told him a number of his experiences in the early community in Jerusalem since the early chapters of Acts strongly reflect Peter's involvement. Traditionally, he is mentioned as being martyred in the persecution instigated by Nero that broke out after the fire in Rome in 65AD.

Philip the Evangelist

Philip the Evangelist was an early Jewish convert to Christianity. His exemplary character in the early church was such that he was selected, as well as six others, to serve as a deacon. Philip, later in his life, married, lived in Caesarea, and was the father of four daughters who possessed the gift of prophecy. Philip and Paul met face to face when the apostle, nearing the end of his third missionary journey, stayed several days at Philip's house in Caesarea. (Acts 6:1 – 6; Acts 21:8).

Porcius Festus

Festus was the fifth procurator of Judea from about 59 to 62, succeeding Antonius Felix. He inherited the problems of his predecessor in regard to the Roman practice of creating civic privileges for Jews. During his administration, Jewish hostility to Rome was greatly inflamed by the civic privileges issue. Feelings were aroused which played an important part in the closely following Jewish War of AD 66. Acts relates that the Apostle Paul had his final hearing before Festus (Acts 24:27). In Acts 25:12, Festus sought to induce Paul to go to Jerusalem for trial; Paul appealed to the emperor. The appeal resulted in Paul being sent to Rome for judgment by the emperor himself, although Festus had difficulty in detailing charges against him (Acts 25-26).

Priscilla (Prisca) and Aquila

Aquila was born in the Roman province of Pontus. He, along with his wife Priscilla, were Jews who converted to Christianity. As a couple, they frequently travelled with Paul. Like Paul, they were tentmakers and met him on his first visit to Corinth. The couple had previously resided in Rome but were expelled along with other Jews and Christians by the Emperor Claudius Caesar. Priscilla's name is often listed before her husband Aquila's name. This may be an indication that she had a stronger personality than her husband or that she was of a higher status socially. Priscilla and Aquila accompanied Paul after he left Corinth and went with him to Ephesus. They stayed in the city when Paul continued his journey to Jerusalem. It is after he left that they met Apollos, an eloquent man whose knowledge they completed by telling him about Jesus. The couple resided in Ephesus long enough to meet Paul again when he returned to the city. When Paul wrote his letter to Corinth, from Ephesus, he sent greetings from the couple and commended their selfless sacrifices for the brethren. The couple stayed loyal to Paul to the very end when many others abandoned him. In his last letter to

Timothy before his death, Paul saluted them and their tireless efforts for the gospel (Acts 18:2, 18, 26; II Corinthians 16:19; Romans 16:3 - 4; II Timothy 4:19).

Publius

Publius was described as the chief man, probably the governor, of Melita, or Malta, who received and lodged Paul and his companions on the occasion of their being shipwrecked off that island. Paul healed the father of Publius of a fever. Publius possessed property in Melita: the distinctive title given to him is "the first" of the island;" and two inscriptions, one in Greek, the other in Latin have been found at Civitavecchia, an inscription found in Malta designates the governor of the island by the same title. Publius may perhaps have been the delegate of the Roman praetor of Sicily, to whose jurisdiction Melita, or Malta, belonged. The Roman martyrologies asserted that he was the first bishop of the island (*De Viris Illust.* xix; Baron, *Annal.* 1, 554; Acts 28:7).

Simon the Pharisee

Simon is mentioned by name in Luke's gospel. This would be significant if he were still known when Luke's gospel was completed. I have imagined he was able to furnish Luke with a lot of material only found in Luke's gospel that is based in the homes of Pharisees in Galilee. I credited him with being a significant eyewitness source (Luke 7:36 – 50).

Theophilus

Luke dedicates both his Gospel and the Acts of the Apostles to a man called Theophilus. It is not known who he was. The *Apostolic Constitutions* (c375AD) say that the first Bishop of Caesarea was Zacchaeus the Tax Collector, followed by Cornelius (possibly Cornelius the Centurion) and Theophilus (possibly the one addressed in the Gospel of Luke). In this story, I have imagined this man residing in Caesarea and allowing Luke to use his home as a place where he could write his two works. Within 150 years, Caesarea had become a major Christian centre where many scholars such as Origen were based. It seems to have been an early centre for manuscript copying and production by the Church (Luke 1:1. Acts 1:1).

Titus

Titus was a Gentile convert to Christianity who was one of Paul's most trusted companions. He is not mentioned at all in Acts. He first appeared with Paul when he accompanied him and Barnabas to Jerusalem. During Paul's extended stay in Ephesus, Titus was sent to Corinth to handle the growing distrust and hostility toward the apostle. Paul met up again with Titus in Macedonia to report their respect for him has been restored. Paul, after he was freed from his imprisonment in Rome, reconnected with Titus to give him instructions regarding the believers on Crete (Titus 1:4 -5). Titus was loyal to the apostle to the end, evangelising Dalmatia and Illyricum during Paul's final stay in Rome before martyrdom. Tradition states Titus died sometime after he turned ninety (Galatians 2:1, 3; II Corinthians 2:13, 7:6, 13 - 14, 8:6, 16, 23, 12:18, 13:14; Titus 1:4, 3:15; II Timothy 4:10).

Timothy

Timothy was born in Lystra, the son of a Gentile father and a Jewish mother. Although his mother's lineage made him a Jew, he was not circumcised at birth. This situation was later rectified by Paul. He first met Paul during his second missionary journey visit to

Lystra. Timothy accompanied Paul on most of his second missionary journey. Timothy was Paul's most trusted and closest friend, and he treated Timothy like a son. Paul believed Timothy was the only person he could trust to care for the churches with the same heart he possessed. The notation found at the end of I Corinthians credits Timothy with helping to copy the epistle. Timothy is also credited, in the end notes of the book of Hebrews, with delivering this epistle to its destination. Timothy stayed faithful to Paul until the very end of his life. II Timothy, the last letter the apostle wrote, shows the faith and love he had for his friend and fellow labourer (Acts 16 to 20; I Thessalonians 1:3; II Thessalonians 1:1; I Corinthians 4:6; II Corinthians 1:1; Romans 16:21; Hebrews 13:23; Philippians 1:2; Colossians 1:1; Philemon 1:1; I Timothy 1:6; II Timothy 1:1).

Trophimus

Trophimus, a Gentile convert to Christianity, was one of the people who accompanied Paul on his return trip from Corinth to Jerusalem. Trophimus' arrival in Jerusalem was noticed by some of the city's Jews who knew he was not Jewish. When Paul visited the temple, the Jews thought he was bringing Trophimus into the temple, an act that was strictly forbidden. Their mistake, coupled with their already existing hatred of the gospel, was the catalyst for a riot that got the apostle arrested by the Romans (Acts 20:4, 21:29; II Timothy 4:20).

Tychicus

Tychicus was from the province of Asia, possibly Ephesus. In his letter to the Ephesians and to the Colossians, Paul calls Tychicus a "dear brother and faithful servant in the Lord." In both Ephesians and Colossians, Paul indicates that he is sending Tychicus to them in order to encourage them. Along with Onesimus, Tychicus took Paul's letter to Colossae. Later references in Paul's letters to Timothy and Titus show that Tychicus was again with Paul after the appeal to the emperor had resulted in him regaining his freedom in Rome. The apostle wrote to Titus, who was in Crete in charge of the churches there, that he intended to send either Artemas or Tychicus to him to take the oversight of the work of the gospel so that Titus might be free to come be with the apostle at Nicopolis. Paul sent Tychicus to Ephesus. As Timothy was in charge of the church in Ephesus, the coming of Tychicus would set him free, so as to enable him to set off at once to re-join Paul at Rome (Acts 20:4; Ephesians 6:21; Colossians 4:7; II Timothy 4:12; Titus 3:12).

Zacchaeus

Zacchaeus is only mentioned in Luke's gospel, so it is likely he met Luke at some point. Zacchaeus met Jesus in Jericho. The *Apostolic Constitutions* (c375AD) say that the first Bishop of Caesarea was Zacchaeus the Tax Collector. Based on this tradition, I placed him in Caesarea and as a key person in assisting both Paul and Lucas (Luke 19:1 – 10).

NOTES

(1) Acts 21:30 - 36
(2) Acts 21:37 - 40
(3) Acts 22:1 - 22
(4) Acts 22:23 - 29
(5) Acts 16:13 - 15
(6) Acts 23:11
(7) The Story of Paul - the Middle Years, Chapter 28. By Trevor Galpin
(8) Acts 23:12 - 22
(9) Acts 23:23 - 32
(10) Acts 23:33 – 35
(11) Luke 19:1 - 10
(12) Acts 2:1 - 5
(13) *The Apostolic Constitutions* (c375AD) says that the first Bishop of Caesarea was Zacchaeus the Tax Collector, followed by Cornelius (possibly Cornelius the Centurion) and Theophilus (possibly the address of the Gospel of Luke).
(14) Acts 24:1 - 22
(15) *Josephus The Jewish War* I, 21, 10; *Antiquities of the Jews XIV*, chapter 13.9)
(16) Acts 24:24 - 26
(17) Luke 3:1- 14
(18) Luke 23:1 - 12
(19) Acts 6:8 - 10

(20) Acts 6:11 - 15
(21) Acts 7:55 - 60
(22) Acts 26:9 - 11
(23) Luke 1:1 - 4
(24) Acts 10:1 - 48
(25) Luke 10:38 -42
(26) Luke 13:31 - 35
(27) Luke 7:11 - 17
(28) Luke 4:14 - 30
(29) Jude 1:1 - 2
(30) Luke 3:23 - 38
(31) Luke 2:41 - 52
(32) Luke 5:17 - 26
(33) Luke 7:36 - 50
(34) Luke 14:1 - 24
(35) Luke 15:1 - 32
(36) Luke 24:13 - 32
(37) Luke 24:33 - 49
(38) Luke 1:1 - 4
(39) Ephesians 1:1
(40) Ephesians 1:3 - 14
(41) Ephesians 1:17 - 18
(42) Ephesians 2:13 - 18
(43) Ephesians 2:19 - 22
(44) Ephesians 3:2 - 6
(45) Ephesians 3:7 - 13
(46) Ephesians 3:14 - 19

(47) Ephesians 3:20 - 21
(48) Ephesians 4:1 - 6
(49) Ephesians 4:17 - 19
(50) Ephesians 4:20 - 24
(51) Ephesians 4:29 - 5:4
(52) Ephesians 5:8 - 20
(53) Ephesians 5:21 - 24
(54) Ephesians 5:25 - 28
(55) Ephesians 6:10 - 20
(56) Ephesians 6:21 - 24
(57) Acts 25:1 - 12
(58) Acts 25:13 - 26:32
(59) Acts 27:1 - 44
(60) Acts 28:1 - 10
(61) Bruce W. Longenecker in his book, *The Crosses of Pompeii. Jesus-Devotion in a Vesuvian Town,* writes the most important Christian place in Pompeii was the bakery in the Insula Arriana Pollians, where a cross was found, in a prominent place on the wall, made from raised plaster. He details many examples of street crosses, which strengthens the other evidence that exists in Pompeii for Christianity.
(62) Longenecker also describes the graffito, found in a large residence (7.11.11), reads, "audi Christianos…" ("listen to the Christians…), and hints at the practice of preaching which was so helped the quick spread of the faith in the Roman world. The Meges ring shows a cross surmounting a symbol for eternal life. Again, a concise summation of

the Christian message. Meges appears to be the name of its owner.

(63) Acts 28:11 - 15.

(64) Acts 28:17 – 28

(65) Tacitus, *The Annals*, passage (15.44) "But all human efforts, all the lavish gifts of the emperor, and the propitiations of the gods, did not banish the sinister belief that the conflagration was the result of an order. Consequently, to get rid of the report, Nero fastened the guilt and inflicted the most exquisite tortures on a class hated for their abominations, called Christians by the populace. Christus, from whom the name had its origin, suffered the extreme penalty during the reign of Tiberius at the hands of one of our procurators, Pontius Pilatus, and a most mischievous superstition, thus checked for the moment, again broke out not only in Judæa, the first source of the evil, but even in Rome, where all things hideous and shameful from every part of the world find their centre and become popular. Accordingly, an arrest was first made of all who pleaded guilty; then, upon their information, an immense multitude was convicted, not so much of the crime of firing the city, as of hatred against mankind."

(66) Tacitus, *Annals*. "Mockery of every sort was added to their deaths. Covered with the skins of beasts, they were torn by dogs and perished, or were nailed to crosses, or were doomed to the flames and burnt, to serve as a nightly illumination, when daylight had expired. Nero offered his

gardens for the spectacle, and was exhibiting a show in the circus, while he mingled with the people in the dress of a charioteer or stood aloft on a car. Hence, even for criminals who deserved extreme and exemplary punishment, there arose a feeling of compassion; for it was not, as it seemed, for the public good, but to glut one man's cruelty, that they were being destroyed."

(67) Titus 1:4 - 5
(68) Titus 3:3 - 7
(69) Titus 3:12 - 13
(70) I Timothy 1:18 - 19
(71) 1 Timothy 5:23
(72) 1 Timothy 6:11 - 12
(73) 2 Timothy 1:3 - 4
(74) 2 Timothy 1:6 - 7; 13 - 14
(75) 2 Timothy 4:1 - 5
(76) 2 Timothy 4:6 - 8
(77) 2 Timothy 4:9 - 13; 19 - 20
(78) Daniel 2:44
(79) According to the *Liber Pontificalis*, Paul's body was buried outside the walls of Rome, at the second mile on the Via Ostiensis, on the estate owned by a Christian woman named Lucina.

OTHER BOOKS BY TREVOR GALPIN

FALLING FROM GRACE - 2ND EDITION
and being caught by the Father (2021)

This book describes Trevor's journey from being a hardworking, wounded, orphan hearted pastor to discovering his true identity as a son of God the Father who is loved unconditionally.

JESUS AND HIS FATHER
by his family and friends (2014)

The revealing of God as Father was the primary ministry of Jesus. He revealed this through conversations with his family and friends. This book is the story of fourteen people who heard Jesus say things about God as a Father as recorded in the Gospels.

FINDING THE FATHER
in the Story of the Church *(2016)*

When Jesus returned to his Father, he commissioned his followers to continue his work. This is the story of how the church has tried to do this through 2000 years. It looks specifically at the place the truth about the Father heart of God has had in the story. Sometimes it was almost forgotten but gloriously has not been lost.

THE STORY OF PAUL
The Early Years *(2018)*

This book sets the scene for the early part of Paul's ministry up to the end of his first missionary journey and his writing of the Letter to the Galatians. It is a theological discussion of Paul's revelation of sonship set against a backdrop of the early events of Paul's life and ministry.

THE STORY OF PAUL PART II
The Middle Years *(2020)*

This book is a fictive historical narrative covering Paul's second and third missionary journeys and the writing of a number of his letters during that period. It explores, in a fictional way, the challenges and struggles of Paul's life as outlined in II Corinthians. It concludes with him being arrested and imprisoned in Caesarea.

THE BIG PICTURE
Finding the Father in the Bible (*2021*)

This book explores, as its title suggests, the great sweep of revelation of the nature of God who has always been Father and how he reveals himself through the pages of the Old and New Testament and the coming of his Son into the world who reconciles us to the Father. It seeks to join together the many elements of teaching on these topics currently circulating like a huge jigsaw puzzle.

**You can contact Trevor Galpin via his website:
www.trevorandlinda.uk**

All the above books are available on Amazon in paperback, Kindle, Book Depository, and by ordering from major book sellers worldwide.

The Story of Paul I – the Early Years is also available as an audio book read by Trevor. It can be obtained from many platforms including Amazon and Audible.

If you wish to discuss any of the issues raised by these books, Trevor can be contacted by email: tlgminsus@gmail.com

RESOURCES

- **Trevor and Linda Galpin's website:**
  www.trevorandlinda.uk
  This website includes Trevor's blog, resources, itinerary and ways of supporting them in their ministry.

- **Father Heart UK:**
  www.fatherheart.uk
  News and events from the Father Heart team in the UK.

- **A Father to You:**
  www.afathertoyou.com
  Mark Gyde's website with lots of audio and video teachings, teaching materials and inspirational videos.

- **Fatherheart Ministries:**
  www.fatherheart.net

- **James and Denise Jordan:**
  www.jordaninternational.net

- **Stephen Hill:**
  www.ancientfuture.co.nz

www.ingramcontent.com/pod-product-compliance
Lightning Source LLC
Chambersburg PA
CBHW030035100526
44590CB00011B/205